The Beer League Hockey Handbook

Steve Duncan

Illustrations by Bob Sherwood

Copyright 2010© Steve Duncan

All Rights Reserved. No part of this publication may be reproduced, stored in a retrieval system, or transmitted in any form by any means, electronic, mechanical, photocopying, recording or otherwise without written permission from the author.
Except for brief quotations embodied in critical articles or reviews.

Printed in Canada

ISBN 978-0-9865412-0-9

FIN 18 10 10

Library and Archives Canada Cataloguing in Publication

Duncan, Steve, 1980-
    The official beer league hockey handbook / Steve Duncan.

ISBN 978-0-9865412-0-9

    1. Hockey--Humor. I. Title.

GV847.D86 2010   796.96202'07   C2010-901317-4

"I believe it was the immortal philosopher Homer Simpson who said, 'It's funny cause it's true'. The Beer League Hockey Handbook is just that. You will recognize pretty much every character in the book. We sometimes take hockey a little too seriously in this country. Steve reminds us all to have a chuckle sometimes...not only at the guy on the bench next to us, but also ourselves".

James Duthie, Host of NHL on TSN

Table of Contents

CHAPTER 1 - *Origin of the Beer League* ....Pg. 3

CHAPTER 2 - *Starting Lineups* ....Pg. 7

CHAPTER 3 - *The Men in Stripes* ....Pg. 81

CHAPTER 4 - *Terms From the Dressing Room* ....Pg. 91

Acknowledgements ....Pg. 99

About the Author ....Pg. 100

CHAPTER 1

Origin of the Beer League

**Beers, the boys, and a whole lot of stories.
This is where it all began...**

Origin of the Beer League

Beer – (noun): The world's oldest and most widely consumed alcoholic beverage and third most popular drink overall after water and tea.
League – (noun): Term commonly used to describe a group of sports teams that compete against one another.
Hockey – (noun): A fast-paced, physical sport in which skaters use sticks to direct a puck into the opposing team's goal.

Put those three together and it sounds pretty fun, doesn't it?

Some call it exercise while others call it a night out with the boys. Whatever the case may be, thousands of people around the world are addicted to the sport of recreational hockey, better known as *"Beer League"*. With players generally aged between 19 and 65, there's just about a Beer League suitable for anybody.

So where does the term "beer" come in to play? Quite honestly, the majority of the players playing in Beer Leagues are more interested in the *post-game pints* than actually playing the game itself. You've maybe heard the expression: "We're a beer drinking team with a hockey problem". That's the case with many teams, which is why the name – *Beer League Hockey*, couldn't be more accurate.

WHERE IT ALL BEGAN:

The first ever recreational indoor hockey game took place on March 3rd, 1875, at the Victoria Skating Rink in Montreal, Canada. Organized by James Creighton (a Canadian Engineer, Journalist, and Lawyer), the two teams consisting of McGill University students, skated nine against nine, and used a wooden puck. Creighton felt that if they used a ball, it could potentially fly out of play and injure the spectators as there were no boards on the rink. The teams battled for 60 minutes in hopes of scoring on their opposition's goal made up of two metal pegs and separated six feet apart. And would you believe it? Following the game, a fight broke out between the players and the spectators.

Some things never change do they?

Since the inaugural game was played in Montreal, hockey leagues have been forming by the hundreds both professionally and recreationally worldwide. And now well over a century later, the game of hockey has evolved into one of the most popular sports in the world and still continues to grow.

There are so many aspects of Beer League Hockey that players fall in love with. Many will tell you that it's their escape from reality. You could be having the worst day at the office or trouble at home with the kids, but when you come to the rink – all is forgotten. That hour of ice-time and night out with the guy's is your most cherished time of the week. Ahh, you've got to love the passion!

THE DRESSING ROOM:

The room in which memories are shared (and stored) is one of the most beloved aspects of Beer League Hockey. Remarkably, you've sat in the hockey dressing room for the 500th time and yet there's still something new that takes place that you've never seen or heard before. The dressing room really brings out the best in everyone. If you can't have a laugh in the room, then you're not wanted on the team. It really doesn't matter how good or bad you are, it's all about who you are off the ice. The dressing room talk is the most sacred part of the game, and its tradition and stories will live on for generations to come.

On some nights, players spend more time in the dressing room than they do on the ice....well, most nights actually. Before the game, players get caught up with one another, while after the game, it's all about sitting back and talking hockey and enjoying a cold one (or two...well, three). What better way to enjoy time out with your buddies?

THE GAME:

"What did we sign up for again? Oh right, to play hockey".

Teams will hit the ice for three periods of bumping and bruising and a whole lot of action. These guys aren't professional by any means, but they can put on quite a show. Games will be filled with a little bit of everything, from memorable saves to highlight reel goals to even the occasional fight or two.

Through Beer League's around the world there is an old expression - "Leave it on the ice!" Players may downright hate each other on the ice, but once the game is over, you shake hands and go back to your dressing room. On many occasions you'll find two players that dropped their gloves in their previous game sitting together enjoying a beer afterwards. It's a true testament to the level of respect that players have with one another on and off the ice....well, in most cases that is.

There may only be two or three people in the stands, but to some Beer League player's there might as well be 20,000 screaming fans. It's a long season, and despite all of the off-ice shenanigans that take place each week, deep down each team wants to take home the title. Beer League represents competition at its finest.

THE AFTERMATH:

As a wise man once said after a loss - "Win or lose, we booze!" Beer League teams live and die by this phrase. Maybe there's a big playoff game on TV that night, or perhaps it's your pal's 30th birthday? Whatever the case may be, the guys will always find a reason to go out and have some fun after their big game. 6:30am is going to come awfully early the next day! And can you believe it? It's all about to happen again next week!

CHAPTER 2

Starting Lineups

A closer look at the characters
that grace beer league rinks around the world...

Starting Lineups

1) "The Great One"..................11
2) "The Has-Been"...................12
3) "What's His Name?"...............13
4) "The Phony"......................14
5) "The Head-Hunter"................15
6) "The Tardy Goalie"...............16
7) "Mr. Cooperalls".................17
8) "The Ringer"....................18
9) "The Neon Guy"..................19
10) "The Scotty Bowman".............20
11) "The Lumberjack"................21
12) "The Ovechkin"..................22
13) "The Old-Timer".................23
14) "The Goon".....................24
15) "Mr. Excuses"..................25
16) "The Mullet"...................26
17) "Mr. Uncomfortable"............27
18) "The Organizer"................28
19) "The Sieve"....................29
20) "The Story-Teller".............30
21) "The Klima"....................31
22) "The Kid".....................32
23) "The Dirt-Bag"................33
24) "Mr. Serious".................34
25) "The Ladies Man"..............35
26) "The Try-Hard"................36
27) "The Die-Hard"................37
28) "Can't Buy One"...............38
29) "The Angry Guy"...............39
30) "The Ugly Guy"................40
31) "Mr. Forgetful"...............41
32) "The Stat-tracker"............42
33) "The Smoker".................43
34) "The Name Dropper"...........44
35) "# 69".......................45

36) "The Pylon"...................46
37) "The Wall"....................47
38) "The Drunk Guy"...............48
39) "Mr. Glass"...................49
40) "The Straggler"...............50
41) "The Celebrator"..............51
42) "The Escape Artist"...........52
43) "The Chick"...................53
44) "The Puck-Hog"................54
45) "The Ice-Hog".................55
46) "The Borrower"................56
47) "Meet Me Outside".............57
48) "The Cherry-Picker"...........58
49) "The Trainer"................59
50) "The Diver"..................60
51) "Mr. Superstitious"..........61
52) "The Angry Goalie"..........62
53) "The Big Guy"................63
54) "The Follower"..............64
55) "The Spaz"..................65
56) "The Naked Guy".............66
57) "The Chirper"...............67
58) "The Lazy Guy"..............68
59) "Mr. Sportsmanship".........69
60) "The Instigator"............70
61) "The Stache"................71
62) "The Shot-Blocker"..........72
63) "The Recruiter".............73
64) "Mr. Giveaway"..............74
65) "The Bobby Orr".............75
66) "Mama's Boy"................76
67) "The Veteran"...............77
68) "The Rental Goalie".........78
69) "The Legend"................79
70) "The Stud"..................80

"The Great One"

For hockey fans of any generation and for sports fans of any kind - it doesn't take a genius to identify the number donned by the greatest hockey player of all time: #99 himself, Wayne Gretzky. Here's a little background of Wayne: He holds over 60 NHL records, has won four Stanley Cups with the Edmonton Oilers, and is the only player in history to score 200 points in a single season. With that said, the sweater number "99" was retired by the National Hockey League in respect to Wayne - commonly known as "The Great One".

Someone forgot to remind Beer League players of this.

"The Great One" is the guy that proudly sports the number 99 each and every time he steps on the ice. Someone needs to ask this guy - "Have you seen yourself play?" Here's some friendly advice: Do yourself a favour and put that jersey back in your bag because in about five minutes, the other team will be making fun of you.

To sum it up - "The Great One" really isn't great at all. In fact, he's one of the worst skaters on the ice. This player actually has the ability to single-handedly ruin his team on any given night. Rest assured, the moment this guy messes up, the opposing team will be all over him. You'll often hear such expressions as - "At-a-boy, Wayne" or "Good job out there, Gretz!" The unfortunate thing about "The Great One" is the poor guy doesn't realize how terrible he really is. Sorry Wayne!

Oh well, what's a Beer League hockey game without an easy target to make fun of?

Player's skill level: 2*
Player's likeability in the dressing room: 3*

*Ratings based on a scale of 1-10

"The Has-Been"

Typically the guy that could do no wrong back in his high school days, "The Has-Been" is the player that had all the skill in the world, but just never knew how to apply himself.

"The Has-Been" had played some high caliber hockey growing up. The problem with this player is he let all of the fame and glory go to his head.

"Hmm, do I go to practice, or do I hang out with one of my new girlfriends?"

That's an easy answer. The mentality of "The Has-Been" was (and usually still is) girls, partying, and booze. This guy always just wanted to live the life rather than take what could have been a professional hockey career to the next level.

The great thing about this Beer League classic? He's one of the best guys to have on your roster. Not only does he still have talent, but he's a blast in the dressing room and loves to party after the game.

When asking "The Has-Been" if throwing his hockey career out the window for the life he ended up with was worth it, you'll receive one answer:

"Absolutely".

Player's skill level: 9
Player's likeability in the dressing room: 9

"What's His Name?"

It's funny when you're sitting on the bench during the 20th game of your season, and you still don't have a clue what the name of the guy sitting next to you is. Simply put, he's the "What's His Name?"

The big question on everybody's mind is - "How is this guy even on our team?" Typically, the "What's His Name?" has some form of connection with the team ie: he's the brother-in-law of the best friend of your goalie's fiancée...you get the point.

Now on every Beer League team, there are often changes in the off-season. A player can't afford to pay, perhaps two players moved away, maybe a new-born is keeping your former star player off the roster? Well, this is where the "What's His Name?" weasels his way in. He's more then happy to fill that roster spot and will show up to the rink nice and early with his money in hand.

Now in fairness to this Beer League player, he had more than likely introduced himself at the beginning of the season, but hey, you're talking to a room full of Beer League hockey players, pal! By the fifth or sixth week of play, when nobody *still* remembers his name, it simply becomes too embarrassing to even bother asking him at this point. It's funny that his teammates would rather refer to him by his jersey number than actually trying to figure out who he is. "Go #16, you've got it buddy!"

Poor guy. Oh well, everybody deserves a chance to play. Next season, just tell this guy to bring a name tag.

Player's skill level: 3
Player's likeability in the dressing room: N/A (no one has actually ever talked to him)

"The Phony"

"Yeah, I'm going to try out the new *Vapor 8000*...not even on the shelves yet!"

That's the type of comment you'll typically hear from this guy. "The Phony" is an interesting character, and you'll usually find a guy like this floating around one or two teams over the course of a season.

"The Phony" is the guy who has all of the top of the line gear. He'll show up to the dressing room 45 minutes before the game with a couple of brand new $300 sticks. He'll bust out his $200 dry-fit shirt, just before pulling out his $250 gloves that he purchased on E-Bay. He'll lace up his $800 skates that his Bauer-rep friend gave him for 1/2 price. His gear is now strapped on and ready to go. He's set to take the ice after his pre-game stretch in the dressing room. He grabs his bottle filled with the latest energy drink, picks up his shiny new twig, and heads out for warm-up. He steps on the ice, drops a few pucks down, and is ready to play...

Too bad this guy sucks!

"The Phony" is all glamour, and no skill. He likes to think that he's the best player on the ice, but is truly one of the worst players out there. Sadly, "The Phony" talks a big game but by no means can back it up. Not only does he fool you with his appearance, but he'll fool you into thinking that he's a great player. That is of course until you see him out there.

Oh well, at least he looks good in the dressing room.

Player's skill level: 2
Player's likeability in the dressing room: 3

"The Head-Hunter"

LOOK OUT!

He's the guy that tees up a shot any chance he can get. "The Head-Hunter" is the Beer League player that has a bullet of a shot, but absolutely no control over it.

The unfortunate thing about "The Head-Hunter" is that he barely scores. Yeah, he has a hell of a shot, but it's too bad he's not shooting on a soccer net.

He's even his own goalie's worst enemy. While warming up his keeper, he's the guy that will ding him off the mask.

Buddy, keep the shots down, would ya?

"The Head-Hunter" is not afraid to unload his cannon as soon as the puck is on his stick. When playing defence, he'll tee up a shot and rattle it off the glass. As an opposing player, you best not get in the way of this, unless you're planning a visit to the hospital.

If he happens to put the puck in the net, it's usually a pretty nice goal. But don't expect too much from this guy over the course of the season, other than a few broken ribs and a couple of missing teeth.

Player's skill level: 5
Player's likeability in the dressing room: 6

"The Tardy Goalie"

"Is he coming??"

"Ya, he's coming! You know Jerry, he's always late!"

He's the guy that gives everybody a nervous breakdown five minutes before the game. He of course is "The Tardy Goalie".

Goalies often forget that they're the most important players on the ice. If one of your defenceman or forwards can't make it - oh well! Without your goalie, the entire game is ruined and your opposing team will hate you for it.

"The Tardy Goalie" really doesn't have a good reason for not making it on time. Quite simply, he leaves his house 15 minutes before the game. Teammates will curse and rant about him prior to his arrival, but once he shows up, you've got a room full of happy hockey players.

"The Tardy Goalie" is often a pretty good tender. He's pretty relaxed between the pipes because he never really has a chance to think about the up-coming game. Although be careful when he's *really* late, as he will miss warm-up all together, and the opposing team will take full advantage of this by firing all kinds of shots at him early.

He'll keep you guessing, but he'll never let you down. "The Tardy Goalie" will give Beer League teams a chance on every given night. Someone just needs to get this guy an alarm clock!

Player's skill level: 6
Player's likeability in the dressing room: 7

"Mr. Cooperalls"

Remember these beauties? The Cooperalls are a piece of discontinued ice hockey equipment, which were made famous by the hockey manufacturer *Cooper* back in the early 1980's. Now close to some 30 years later, the Cooperalls still grace the occasional hockey bag across the world.

Simply put - "Mr. Cooperalls" is the guy that wears with pride one of the most authentic pieces of hockey apparel you'll ever see. This player will usually receive a reaction such as:

"Wow - look at those bad boys! Classic!"

Now it should be noted that there are actually two types of "Mr. Cooperalls":

1) The guy that wants to bring back the retro look, and enjoys a reaction out of his teammates
2) The guy that's too cheap to buy a modern day hockey pant

Regardless of which guy it is, "Mr. Cooperalls" is one character you love to see on the ice, and he's always there for a good laugh over the course of the season.

Player's skill level: 3
Player's likeability in the dressing room: 9 (How can't you love a guy sporting those things?)

"The Ringer"

You'll only see this guy once playoffs arrive. "The Ringer" is the Beer League star that gets picked up by a team once their regular season is over and the games *really count!*

"The Ringer" simply should NOT be playing Beer League Hockey. He's a player that got put out of the playoffs in his Professional Hockey League, and is back home until next season's training camp. As soon as a League Captain finds out he's home, they're quickly on the phone with him.

"Mikey – I heard you're back in town, man – tough loss the other night....so do you wanna play for our team tonight?"

This player is despised by his opponents, and rightfully so. According to "The Stat-Tracker" (see pg. 42) "The Ringer's" team played it's opposition five times over the regular season and lost by at least eight goals during every contest. Now he joins the team and they win 5-4? Not cool!

Teams will try and get away with inserting this player into their line-up, but will rarely succeed in doing so, as opposing teams will protest. His team will make up a fake name for him on the scoresheet, or will give him another player's jersey. Come on, guys – who are you trying to fool here?

Games involving "The Ringer" will usually result in a forfeit, but hey, it was worth a shot! Now don't forget to pay him the $20 you promised.

Player's skill level: 10
Player's likeability in the dressing room: 8

"The Neon Guy"

We're all grown men out there, right?!...Right?!...So what's up with the pink laces?

Beer Leagues around the globe have dealt with this guy since the first appearance of the neon laces back in the early 1980's. "Mr. Neon" is the guy that's very happy to support the local sports gimmick stores while maintaining his "I don't give a $@#&" attitude on the ice. The trend is still somewhat popular in youth hockey organizations...but did I mention we're all grown men out there?

But it doesn't just stop with the laces! "Mr. Neon" has no boundaries. This guy will sport any type of colourful materials that are on the market, from green neon stick tape to bright orange jerseys. This guy has no shame.

Now don't be fooled! "Mr. Neon" can often be a cover. When opposing players first see this guy their initial impression is - "Look at this pansy in the hot-pink laces". But it has been known that "Mr. Neon" strategically wears these colours as a distraction, and often turns out to be one of the better players on the ice. (Works as a great in-*your*-face tactic to your opposition as well). "You just got schooled by a guy with pink laces!"

In most instances however, this poor guy really has no clue and actually thinks that his neon gear is cool.

His harmless attempt at whatever the heck he's trying to attempt, usually calls for a good discussion in the dressing room. Opposing players will hate you, which is why "Mr. Neon" can be such a menace throughout Beer Leagues across the world.

Player's skill level: 2 *or* 10
Player's likeability in the dressing room: 7

"The Scotty Bowman"

"Come on boys, let's go now! We've gotta take it to 'em! Let's dig deep, give it everything we've got!"

Would you please shut the $%# up!

"The Scotty Bowman" is the guy that does not stop talking on the bench. Some may also refer to this guy as the "Know-It-All".

Now don't get me wrong, everybody loves the **REAL** Scotty Bowman....but yeah, that's because he was a great **NHL** coach...you know, that Professional Hockey League in which players get *paid* to play?!

Although sometimes an asset to his teammates, "The Scotty Bowman" is actually more annoying than helpful. Someone needs to remind this guy that it's a Beer League, and that the most important thing is figuring out what type of draught you'll be drinking after the game. The fact is, this guy doesn't mean to be annoying, and he's generally pretty close with the rest of the teammates. But once this player gets to the rink, he should really be showing up in a shirt and tie.

After the game, the problems continue with "The Scotty Bowman" as coaching strategies are discussed in the dressing room right up until the last player leaves. This post-game discussion is all about "what we did wrong" and "how we could have won the game!"

Hey bud, if we wanted a coach, we would have hired one.

Player's skill level: 6
Player's likeability in the dressing room: 4

"The Lumberjack"

TIMBER!!!!

This is what players should scream when this character hits the ice. "The Lumberjack" is the Beer League player that actually forgets that his hockey stick is not an axe. He will chop and smash his way for three periods on any given night.

Remember when your first hockey coach taught you to "Keep your stick on the ice?" Well, this guy must have called in sick that day.

"The Lumberjack" is usually a decent player on a Beer League roster. His problem is, he just wants to win so bad, that he'll swing at anything in his way to make that happen. He has developed such a style of play, that it's to the point that he doesn't even realize he's doing it anymore. The second he delivers a nice two-hander across his opponent's shin pads, the referee's hand will go up signaling for a penalty. His immediate response: "What did I do?"

There's always room for this player on a Beer League roster. An overall pretty good guy to have on your team, the "Lumberjack" will proudly live on for generations of Beer Leagues to come.

Player's skill level: 5
Player's likeability in the dressing room: 7

"The Ovechkin"

Every Beer League player wants to be the best player on the ice. So why not just mimic one of the best players in the world today?

"The Ovechkin" goes all out to replicate the *real* Alexander Ovechkin night in and night out. You'll often see this player sporting the following "Ovechkinesque" items:

- yellow wax laces
- smoked visor
- #8 on the jersey
- strings on hockey pants exposed and hanging
- massive shoulder pads
- scruffy beard

When scoring a goal (which is rare for this wannabe) he has actually been known to jump into the glass imitating his idol. Did somebody remind this guy that the only person in the stands is the guy mopping the floors?

"Ahh, so if I look like Ovechkin, and feel like Ovechkin, I'm going to play like him, right?

Wrong!

"The Ovechkin" spends so much time trying to look like his idol that it takes away from the way he actually plays, causing him to be one of the crappiest players on the ice.

Now if this guy shows up to the room one week with a missing tooth, then we really have a problem.

Player's skill level: 3
Player's likeability in the dressing room: 5

"The Old-Timer"

Playing in Beer League's since the 1950's, "The Old-Timer" is one of the all-time classic players to lace up the skates.

The great thing about "The Old-Timer" is every league has at least one of him. Whether he's a grandfather of a teammate or maybe a great uncle, teams will always leave room for this beloved character. Not only is he loved by his teammates, but he's well respected by his opponents around the league.

In many instances, this player can barely walk, but once you throw a pair of skates on him, he doesn't stop moving! Teammates will always do their best to get "The Old-Timer" the puck as there's no player on the ice that they would rather see put the puck in the back of the net then him.

Not only is he great on the bench, but he's always happy to treat the boys to a beer after the game. Not to mention he's got a ton of great stories that would even make "The Story-Teller" proud. (See pg. 30)

This guy will tell you when helmets were for sissies. A treat to have on any Beer League roster, "The Old-Timer" is one of the all-time greatest.

Player's skill level: 2
Player's likeability in the dressing room: 10

"The Goon"

Also commonly known as "The Meathead", "The Goon" is one of the toughest players you will ever find in Beer League Hockey.

Essentially "The Goon" is a player that has no hockey sense whatsoever. He can barely skate, and it'll be a cold day in hell before he buries a goal, but when it comes to taking somebody out, he's your man. This guy can swing his fists with the best of them and will never hesitate to drop the gloves with an opposing player.

"The Goon" is out there for one thing: To make the other team's lives miserable. You get in his path, and he'll knock you down. He doesn't care about the two minutes in the box, he's just happy that he sent you back to the bench holding your neck.

Ask "The Goon" what his favourite movie is, and he'll tell you "Slapshot". There's always a good chance that you'll see him doing his best "Reg Dunlop" impression in the dressing room.

He's the guy you hate to play against, but love to have on your roster. Another one of the all-time classic characters, "The Goon" will always have your back...that is if he's not busy breaking someone else's.

Player's skill level: 3
Player's likeability in the dressing room: 9

"Mr. Excuses"

Ever heard of the term - "He's full of excuses?" Well, that expression was created because of this Beer League pain in the @$$.

"Mr. Excuses" is the player that can never admit to making a mistake, as he always has to blame something (or someone) else.

"The ice is crap tonight - it's impossible to control the puck!"
"Man, I just can't get used to this new stick, the curve is completely different than my last one!"
"This ref has always had it in for us!"
"I shouldn't have ate that burger and fries before the game!"

That's right. This guy has an excuse for everything. The real problem with "Mr. Excuses" is he's a terrible hockey player. There are players in the league like "The Pylon" (see pg. 46) that struggle out there, but at least they know they struggle. Not this guy. He actually believes that he is a good player, and that everything that goes wrong out there is somebody else's fault.

It's actually quite painful listening to this guy.

"Mr. Excuses" will even resort to blaming his own teammates for his mistakes. Somebody needs to give this guy a reality check. The reason why you didn't score is because *you are garbage!* End of story.

Player's skill level: 2
Player's likeability in the dressing room: 2

"The Mullet"

Why this classic haircut and Beer League Hockey go hand-in-hand is a mystery that has yet to be solved.

"The Mullet" is a hairstyle that is short at the front and sides, and long in the back. It's also a guy that plays on your Beer League hockey team.

Truth be told, "The Mullet" wishes that helmets were never invented, as he would prefer to show off those long....well short....well long locks each game.

As a player, "The Mullet" is decent at best. He'll work hard for his team each night, and collect a few tap-in goals around the net. (Not much finesse out of this guy!) Sadly he's one of the players that you'll hear getting picked on throughout a game. (See "The Chirper" - pg. 67). But when are players going to realize that chirping him about his hair isn't going to offend him? It's not like his haircut was an accident. He loves his short-long! That's like trash-talking somebody for scoring a nice goal!

When "The Mullet's" elementary school teacher asked him what he wanted to be when he grew up he had two answers: A Professional Wrestler or a Beer League hockey player. Looks like hard work always pays off.

Player's skill level: 5
Player's likeability in the dressing room: 7

"Mr. Uncomfortable"

"You better not be looking at me!"

That's one thing that "Mr. Uncomfortable" will make *very* clear to his teammates if some "inappropriate behaviour" is taking place in the dressing room.

The hockey dressing room has been known to have some *unusual* moments that take place, but this player simply can't handle them. If you've got something *funny* to say, just keep it to yourself when this guy's around.

It's been told that "Mr. Uncomfortable" will be the first one out of the dressing room for the simple fact that he doesn't want to be naked in front of his teammates in case some post-game shenanigans are about to break out. Now there's a very good chance that "Mr. Uncomfortable" is just being paranoid, and no players on the team are actually interested in the guy, but good luck convincing him of this.

On the ice, he's all business. He's a skilled and tough player who is out to win. But even though he's one of the tougher guys on your roster, he's also one of the easiest targets for his teammates to pick on. Being up against a room full of Beer League hockey players, the more he shows his frustration, the more his team will likely try to *expose* him.

Player's skill level: 7
Player's likeability in the dressing room: 6 (10 if you're his friend in the picture)

"The Organizer"

If it wasn't for this guy, Beer League Hockey wouldn't exist.

"The Organizer" (also referred to as "The Captain") is the player that submits his squad into a Beer League each and every season. He orders jerseys, picks the players for his team, comes up with the team name and logo, really this guy does it all. Does he mind? Not a chance. That is until his player's forget to pay him their league fee. (See "The Straggler" - pg. 50).

It's a lot of running around to put together a team, and when talking to "The Organizer" he'll tell you – "It's like another full time job!" But when it comes to Beer League Hockey with this guy, the passion of the game *always* comes first.

Now even though he is "The Captain" and often sports the "C" on his jersey, that doesn't mean that he's the best player on the team. In fact, "The Organizer" is often one of the weaker players on his squad. But hey, he organized the team, so who's complaining, right?

His biggest goal in life is putting together a successful team and bringing home a Championship. Three months before the start of the season, "The Organizer" will get together with "Mr. Serious" (see pg. 34) and "The Recruiter" (see pg. 73) to figure out "who's in" and "who's out" for the season. It's not an easy process, but there will always be a few "cuts" made before their first game. (See "The Follower" - pg. 64).

From "roll call" e-mail blasts, to setting up sponsorships, "The Organizer" will do whatever it takes to make Beer League Hockey a great experience for everyone. Too bad he's not getting paid for it!

Player's skill level: 5
Player's likeability in the dressing room: 8

"The Sieve"

Remember the plastic cut-out shaped goalies that your old man attached to your road hockey net when you were eight years old? Those were better known as the "Mr. Sieve". 30 years later, you'll find yourself shooting on virtually the same thing in Beer Leagues across the world.

"The Sieve" is the crappy goalie in the league that can't stop a beach ball. Essentially, he's as effective between the pipes as a piece of plastic. Heck, there are some Beer League teams that would prefer the piece of plastic over this tender.

Often you'll see *full* benches show up from opposing teams when they know they're playing "The Sieve" as it's going to be a goal-scoring fest. (See "The Stat-Tracker - pg. 42) This is also a great opportunity for some guys to score their first goal of the season. (See "The Pylon" - pg. 46)

"Yes! Johnny's in net tonight!"

So why do teams continue to add these "Sieves" to their rosters? Generally speaking, your goalie is one of the original players on your Beer League squad. He was there when you first put the team together, and now you just can't let him go. (Not to mention he has the goalie equipment!)

At the end of the day, it's not all about winning, and this guy is just happy to be there. "The Sieve" is one of the most loyal players to grace a roster...just try and make a save for Gods Sake!

Player's skill level: 1
Player's likeability in the dressing room: 4

"The Story-Teller"

Somebody hand this guy a microphone!

"The Story-Teller" is the Beer League player that shows up to the dressing room week after week with yet another new story for his teammates.

"You're gonna love this one, fellas!"

"The Story-Teller" loves his hockey. He's one of the better players to have on your Beer League squad as he adds some flavour to the room, as well as being a fairly skilled player. Many of the stories you'll hear from this guy are from "back in the day" with his old hockey teams.

Make sure if you have a story to tell that "The Story-Teller" isn't in the room with you, because he'll shut you down half way through and *one-up* you with a better one. (Teammates will generally learn this half way through the season).

Teammate's girlfriends and wives will often have a problem with "The Story-Teller" as he's always the guy that convinces his players to go out after the game to random spots like the bar or the strip club.

Hey! What's "The Story-Teller" without any stories to tell?

Player's skill level: 7
Player's likeability in the dressing room: 8

"The Klima"

Why is it that every Beer League team has one of these guys? This is the player that refuses to spend $50 on a new helmet. He's better known as "The Klima".

Former NHL'er Petr Klima made these nasty looking buckets famous in the early 1980's. The style of his helmet was big and bulky, and he looked more like an astronaut than a hockey player. I guess some Beer League players still think that this is in style?

"The Klima" is an easy target for other teams. Similar to "The Neon Guy" (see pg. 19), this player gets verbally abused night in and night out from opposing Beer League teams. How does this player rank among the Beer League talent? He's really hit or miss. Sometimes he's a skilled player sporting this look to get a laugh from his teammates, while other times he's just plain awful.

"The Klima" can often go beyond his helmet. You should see the rest of this guy's hockey gear. His gloves have holes in them and smell like roadkill, his hockey pants barely fit him (because he's 50 pounds heavier from the time he bought them), and his skates should be an artifact in the Hockey Hall of Fame.

Bug this guy all you want. But as long as he's in Beer Leagues, rest assured his look will never change.

Player's skill level: 5
Player's likeability in the dressing room: 5

"The Kid"

There are actually two versions of this Beer League character:

1) "The Kid" (Real Version): He's the youngest player on the team, and one of the most talented. "The Kid" is the newest member to join a Beer League, as his days of playing junior hockey are now just a memory.

"The Kid" is a great hockey player, and is often the son of one of the guys on a Beer League team. (Funny that he's not even above the legal drinking age). Regardless, he's happy to be on the team, and his teammates will welcome him in with open arms.

2) "The Kid" (Phony Version): Believe it or not, there is actually an impostor of the real "Kid" - a wannabe so to speak. He's the middle-aged player believing that *he* is still "The Kid". This is just a classic example of how some guys just can't handle getting older. You'll see this guy weaving around in warm-up, trying to pick the puck up on his stick and twirl it around like it's in a lacrosse stick. He'll even try to talk like an 18 year old with comments like "Hey fellas, it's gonna be a gongshow out there tonight!"

Give it a rest, pal. The last time you were "The Kid", *Rock 'Em Sock 'Em Hockey* was coming out on VHS. Hey, no one ever said that it's a bad thing to try and feel and act young, but leave the hot-dogging and high-school jargon at home.

Player's skill level: Real Version 8, Phony Version 6
Player's likeability in the dressing room: Real Version 8, Phony Version 4

"The Dirtbag"

Is it possible that someone could smell just as bad before their game as they do after it? This guy can prove that anything is possible.

"The Dirtbag" is the Beer League hockey player that has absolutely no regard for personal hygiene. He actually sweats for three periods of hockey, heads back to the dressing room, throws his street clothes back on and says "See you next week, boys!"

The term "hit the showers" never really applied to this guy.

It's pretty standard that a hockey player doesn't exactly own a hockey bag that smells too fresh. However, "The Dirtbag" turns it up a notch, and it's not pretty. This player smells so bad that his teammates won't even sit next to him.

Ever smell a flatulence on the hockey bench? Ya, that was him.

As a hockey player, "The Dirtbag" holds his own, but is no superstar to say the least. Let's face it, for gear that smells that bad, he must play a lot of hockey, so he can't be *that* bad!

A dedicated player on any Beer League Roster, "The Dirtbag" is a true classic.

Player's skill level: 5
Player's likeability in the dressing room: 5

"Mr. Serious"

"You think we should call him on the illegal curve?"
"That guy's not a regular player on their roster!"
"Timeout ref! Timeout!"

These are common phrases that come from the mouth of "Mr. Serious".

"Mr. Serious" is the Beer League player that shows up an hour before each game. He wants to make sure that his stick is taped up to perfection, and all of his pre-game stretches are done before the zamboni hits the ice. He also likes to talk strategy before the game with "The Scotty Bowman". (See pg. 20).

Dude, it's Beer League Hockey! Whatever happened to a skate with the boys, followed by a beer after the game? With "Mr. Serious", that's the last thing on his mind.

Did you know that this guy carries a copy of the rule-book in his hockey bag?

"Mr. Serious" is actually a pretty skilled player because he's just so damn into the game. Most Beer League squads will carry one of these characters because of their ability to put the puck in the net. Just try not to lose when this guy's in the line-up or you'll never hear the end of it!

Player's skill level: 7
Player's likeability in the dressing room: 4

"The Ladies Man"

He walks into the rink cool and collected. His hair is slicked back, as he smiles confidently. At first glance you'd think that he just walked into a night-club and not an arena. Following behind him, is one, two, three, maybe even four female companions, admiring every step he takes. Meet "The Ladies Man".

So what's the deal with this guy? "The Ladies Man" is the player on the team that only plays hockey so he can show off his new girlfriend(s) to his buddies at the rink on game night.

"So Mikey – who's the new girl you're with?"
"Ah, just some girl I picked up at the grocery store the other day".

"The Ladies Man" can do it all.

Now if his lady-friends knew anything about the game of hockey or if they were interested in him for his hockey abilities, then he would be leaving the arena by himself on a nightly basis. "The Ladies Man" really doesn't have a clue how to play. Good thing for him is he'll never have to worry about losing a spot on the team, as all the guys love to see who he'll be bringing along each week.

He may look bad on the ice, but off the ice "The Ladies Man" is an all-star in the eyes of his peers.

Player's skill level: 2
Player's likeability in the dressing room: 8

"The Try-Hard"

"Got to get the puck....ungh....I know I can, I know I can!"

Say hello to "The Try-Hard".

This ever-popular player has been seen in Beer League rinks since the beginning of time. To sum this guy up: All heart, no skill.

Teammates have to applaud the efforts of "The Try-Hard". He's the player that gives 100% on every shift, skates hard and never gives up. Problem is, he's never in the play.

To be fair, at times he'll flash some moments of greatness. Often teams will put him on the ice in a penalty-killing situation because he doesn't stop trying.

His best attribute: Battling in the corners.

This guy will work so hard to get the puck off his opposition, that they'll sometimes say "Here - just take it. You obviously want it a lot more then I do!"

His heart is on his sleeve every time he steps on the ice, "The Try-Hard" will stop at nothing to win the game for his team.

Player's skill level: 3
Player's likeability in the dressing room: 7

"The Die-Hard"

Call this guy up 15 minutes before a game, and you know he'll be there. "The Die-Hard" is the guy that NEVER says no to a game of hockey.

"The Die-Hard" is on the ice at least five times a week and plays on three different Beer League teams.

Now the sport of hockey can have a pretty heavy price tag on it, so how can "The Die-Hard" afford all of this? Well, quite frankly, he can't. He just literally spends every penny he has on hockey.

"The Die-Hard" has been known to drive over three hours just to play an hour of pick-up hockey...with no goalies!

"Hey, it's ice time!"

He's one of the good guys in the dressing room, and is one of the better-than-average players on your roster. (Well he better be if he's playing five times a week!) This quality player is also the guy that looks at putting his Beer League team into every hockey tournament that comes by the rink.

If you ever need a last minute substitution, keep this guy on speed dial. "The Die-Hard" will never let you down!

Player's skill level: 6
Player's likeability in the dressing room: 7

"Can't Buy One"

He's a talented part of his Beer League roster and a great all-around team player that can handle the puck, skate, pass, and play both ends of the ice. It's a shame that he can't find the back of the net.

Also referred to as "Stone-hands", "Can't Buy One" is the guy that just can't seem to find a way to score. He's always on the doorstep and has a ton of opportunities, but the end result is either a save, a missed shot, or a big "ping" off the iron.

"Mr. Superstitious" (see pg. 61) will tell him that he needs to get a new stick, but "Can't Buy One" will tell you that he's just not getting the bounces.

Oddly enough, some of the worst players on the team will manage to pop a goal in before this guy. (See "The Pylon" - pg. 46)

"Just give me one, would ya!?"

"Can't Buy One" is a frustrated individual, but is still a great player to carry on your roster, as he brings it each night. But if you're down by a goal with a minute left, you'd best leave him on the bench.

Player's skill level: 6
Player's likeability in the dressing room: 6

"The Angry Guy"

Also referred to as "The Ref hater", "The Angry Guy" is the Beer League player who is pissed off at the world.

There's really no pleasing this guy. He shows up to the rink after a bad day of work, possibly a fight with his wife, maybe his car broke down earlier that morning? The fact of the matter is - you won't hear one positive thing out of this player.

"The Angry Guy" has a reputation around the league. Once the referees step out on the ice, their first reaction when seeing him is - "Ugh, not this guy again!" And rightfully so. "The Angry Guy" is on the referee's backs for three full periods, keeping them up-to-date on just how terrible they are at doing their job. Come on, we all know it's the referee's fault when a team loses a hockey game, right?!

Relax buddy, it's just a game!

Some guys forget that they are playing Beer League Hockey, and it's not the end of the world if a ref misses an offside call during an 11-1 game. Try convincing the "The Angry Guy" of that.

This critic seems to know the rules better than anyone, yet sadly, he's one of the worst players on the team.

From "F-Bombs" to mother insults, "The Angry Guy's" got them all. Just make sure your kids stay home when playing against this guy.

Player's skill level: 4
Player's likeability in the dressing room: 3

"The Ugly Guy"

What can you say about this poor guy? This Beer League player is simply known as "The Ugly Guy".

In Beer League games, teams will often come up with quick names for their opposition to identify them ie: the "monster on defence", or the "kid with the quick hands". Often teams will refer to their opponents by the numbers on their back. "Hey watch out for #7!"

Not this guy!

He's not a popular enough player that every team will carry, however, there's usually one of "The Ugly Guy" hanging around Beer Leagues.

Now players aren't necessarily trying to be mean when talking about this player. How else are they supposed to describe him? "The guy with the uni-brow? The broken nose? The missing teeth?" Call him "The Ugly Guy" and *everybody* will know who you're talking about.

So how exactly does this player rank on the skill chart? Well, he's taken about 50 pucks to the face, so he's a fantastic defensive player. He's brought so much attention to his ugly mug that opposing goalies are distracted, allowing his teammates to produce more goals. Other than that, you really never know what you're going to get with this guy.

Hey, whatever helps pull out a win, right?

Player's skill level: 5
Player's likeability in the dressing room: 5

"Mr. Forgetful"

"Hey man, do you have an extra shin pad?"

Say hello to "Mr. Forgetful".

This guy has been gracing Beer Leagues for years. "Mr. Forgetful" is the player who always manages to forget *something* in his hockey bag. Whether it's a skate or an elbow pad, "Mr. Forgetful" will never have his full set of gear with him.

Now how does something like this happen so often? Usually "Mr. Forgetful" will tell you that he was "drying out his equipment" and must not have loaded up his entire bag. OK fine, but this happens every week! This player becomes a bit of a nuisance to have on a Beer League roster as he always has to hit up his teammates for some extra gear.

"Dude, I'm not lending you my cup!"

It also goes beyond just leaving some of his gear at home. "Mr. Forgetful" will break his stick the week before, and then forget to pick up a new one before his next game. His dull skates will sit in his hockey bag for weeks without sharpening. He's also known for forgetting his wallet so he can't buy a drink after the game. (See "The Straggler" - pg. 50).

Someone should remind him that he's been forgetting to put the puck in the net. "Mr. Forgetful" is one of the guys on the roster that struggles on a nightly basis. Too bad he doesn't forget to show up.

Player's skill level: 3
Player's likeability in the dressing room: 4

"The Stat-Tracker"

"Come on ref, I assisted on that one!"

These are common words from one of Beer League's finest - "The Stat-Tracker".

This player *loves* to track his own points. He will always make sure that the referees credit him for each and every point that he's in on. Once a point is missed, you better believe that somebody's going to hear about it.

Sorry to burst your bubble dude, but there are no scouts in the stands!

Remarkably the knowledge of "The Stat-Tracker" goes beyond his own personal statistics. This player can tell you the final scores of each and every game, who scored the goals, and what the weather was like that night on the way to the arena.

"The Stat-Tracker" is a decent player, but cares way more about his personal performance than the team actually winning.

"I scored a hat-trick tonight, honey!" Ya, that's great stuff pal, but you also lost the game 12-4.

Make sure this guy gets the gamesheet - it's going straight to the fridge!...

Player's skill level: 6 or 60% or .600
Player's likeability in the dressing room: 4

"The Smoker"

As soon as the game is over, he's the first one into the change room. Why? So he can rush to his bag and grab his pack of cigarettes. He's none other than "The Smoker".

Now lots of Beer League players smoke, but this guy is itching for one in between periods! And look pal, If you're going to light one up, do you have to do it in a stuffy change room with 14 other guys? It's worse than a Bingo Hall in there!

The funny thing is "The Smoker" always manages to sit next to the guy that hates smoke the most.

"Yo buddy, put that $#%& out!"

It's interesting how the sport of Beer League Hockey and smoking even go hand in hand. What's wrong with waiting until you're outside like anywhere else?

For the most part, "The Smoker" struggles on the ice. (Surprised?) He's got *some* talent, but his wheels just don't turn like they used to. He'll usually just float around the ice looking for a pass.

30 second shifts are asking a lot out of this guy, although he doesn't mind. He's just out for a skate with the boys because the lungs just can't handle playing hard anymore.

I guess a pack a day and an hour of hockey just don't mix!

Player's skill level: 4
Player's likeability in the dressing room: 6 (1 if you're sitting next to him)

"The Name-Dropper"

A real nuisance to have on the team, "The Name-Dropper" is the guy that just so happens to know every big name in the sport of hockey.

This Beer Leaguer likes to refer to professional hockey players using the nicknames that *their* teammates would call them.

Examples: Iginla = Iggy, Shanahan = Shanny, Bertuzzi = Bert

Newsflash pal - *these guys are not your friends!* Just because you spotted one of these players out in public, doesn't mean you know them!

The "Name-Dropper" is also known for interrupting other people's stories to tell you about his experience with a famous professional player.

"So I was coming down the wing with the puck, and then --" "So ya, me and my buddies were out with 'Vinny' one night - man what a character!"

Hold on - let me correct you on that one: "You and your buddies who are friends with a guy that knows Vincent Lecavalier were out one night". Now stop dropping names!

So what's the caliber of this player? 9 times out of 10, he'll be one of the worst players on your team.

The bottom line is this: Nobody cares about this guy's boring stories talking about people he wishes he could be friends with.

Player's skill level: 3
Player's likeability in the dressing room: 2

It was funny the first time somebody wore it, but now it's just getting old. "# 69" is the player that simply wears the number 69 on the back of his jersey.

In short, the term "69" is something that you learned about on the back of a bathroom stall door.

The odd thing about this player? He actually thinks he's being original by sporting this number. "Ha, no one ever thought of this one!"

Believe it or not, you can really tell the quality of a player by the number on their back. Similar to "The Great One" (see pg. 11), "The 69" is not a very good player at all, and he's actually one of the more annoying guys on the team. Wearing a number like this is just grounds for other teams to make fun of him during the course of a game.

You'll often see a few of these characters on the ice over the course of a season. When they mess up, there are a lot of "insert jokes here" that you'll hear from his opposition.

Someone needs to tell this guy to get rid of this number! It's getting way too easy out there!

Player's skill level: 4
Player's likeability in the dressing room: 4

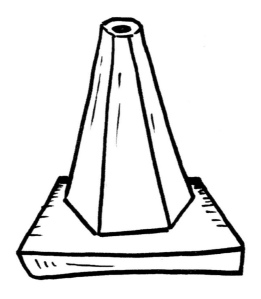

It's probably the term that every hockey player in the world would least like to be labeled as. That of course is "The Pylon".

Typically an item used for running hockey drills, "The Pylon" is essentially the guy that players are "skating circles" around.

By far the worst player on your team, "The Pylon" really shouldn't even be playing in a Beer League. He's so bad, that it's next to impossible for him to even stay on his feet.

Then why do teams put this guy on their roster? The answer is simple: Players like this guy. He generally knows that his on-ice abilities lack worse then a five year old house league player, but he's good friends with everyone on the team.

If "The Pylon" were ever to score a goal, it would be the equivalent of a golfer making a hole-in-one. No, really. Teammates around the Beer League world do everything they can to get him his first goal, including shot attempts off his shin pads, hoping the puck will bounce into the back of the net.

Hey, they all count!

He's great for the dressing room, but a disaster on the ice, although there's no such thing as a Beer League team without him. Just remember to tell him to take his skate guards off before stepping on the ice next time!

Player's skill level: 1
Player's likeability in the dressing room: 8

He's one of the most valuable players on his Beer League team. "The Wall" is the Beer League goalie that stands on his head each night, keeping the puck out of the back of the net.

Ask any player in the league about him, and they'll admit that he's tough to beat. His teammates love him as he gives them a chance to win every single game because of his solid play between the pipes.

You'll sometimes find "The Wall" on Beer League teams that are pretty terrible (which is why they recruited him in the first place). His team will win games 2-1 but they got out-shot 55-20.

Should a strong Beer League team recruit this guy, then it's pretty much game over. "The Wall" has been seen on quite a few teams who take home the Championship. These teams don't usually worry about playing much defense with this guy behind him which is why they can rack up a ton of goals.

"The Wall" is always very modest about his play as well. Tell him that he played a great game, and he'll just nod politely.

A true gentleman and amazing player to have on your roster, "The Wall" is the MVP of Beer Leagues worldwide...

...now go buy him a beer - he just stopped 70 shots for you!

Player's skill level: 10
Player's likeability in the dressing room: 9

"The Drunk Guy"

It's almost surprising that this guy can put his gear on properly. "The Drunk Guy" is the Beer League player that can barely stand up on the ice due to too much alcohol consumption.

It's a beautiful thing to watch as "The Drunk Guy" warms up before the game without a clue as to where he is. He does his best to disguise it ("I've only had a couple") but his teammates all know how sauced he really is.

Remarkably in games, you can actually smell this guy across the other side of the ice.

Some common traits about "The Drunk Guy":
1) He is always good for at least one puke session on the bench per game
2) He will fall down at least once on every shift
3) He gets lippy with the other team for no apparent reason
4) The referee will give him the boot before the game is over
5) At least once in the season, he will sneak a full cooler into the dressing room
6) His water bottle has been filled with beer (sometimes vodka)

He's the player that puts the true meaning into Beer League Hockey, "The Drunk Guy" is one of the *hiccup* all-time classics.

Player's skill level: 3 (depending on whether or not he can see)
Player's likeability in the dressing room: 8

"Mr. Glass"

This player spends more time at the hospital than he does at the rink.

"Mr. Glass" is the guy that always seems to be in the wrong place at the wrong time. This unfortunate player has a grocery list of injuries from pucks to the face to slap shots to the groin. You name it, and it's happened to this player. When's he ever going to catch a break?

In a 30 game Beer League season, "Mr. Glass" is lucky if he plays eight games for you. Once he's back from a three-week injury, you're throwing him right back on the IR because he took a mean slash and broke his wrist.

Even though he misses a ton of games, "Mr. Glass" is one of the beloved players in the dressing room. His teammates always give him a hard time about the bad luck he faces every season.

The great thing about "Mr. Glass" is he always stays optimistic. If the Doctor tells him to stay off the ice for six weeks, you can count on him being back in four.

No one really knows just how good this player is because every time he's on the ice, he's playing hurt. Did anybody ever think to tell him that it's not safe to play with a broken ankle?

To sum him up, "Mr. Glass" has dedication. Even when he's out of the line-up, he'll still show up after the game for a beer. Isn't that what it's really all about? Just make sure he keeps his helmet on in case the floor's wet.

Player's skill level: 5-8 (depending on how badly he's hurt!)
Player's likeability in the dressing room: 8

"The Straggler"

"Hey I forgot my wallet at home, is it cool if I pay you next week?"

He's every Captain's worst nightmare. (See "The Organizer - pg. 28). "The Straggler" is the Beer League player that has every excuse in the world when it comes to paying his hockey fees.

Generally teams will carry "The Straggler" because he's a fantastic player. Captains often front the money for him to play, and at times it takes him the whole season to finally pay in full.

That is *if* "The Straggler" even decides to pay him.

He's a great guy in the room, he puts the puck in the net, and he'll even set up a few nice goals. Too bad he's such a tight-wad! When it comes to excuses "The Straggler" is the king of them. When asked for money, this player has unlimited excuses that he'll throw your way.

Examples:
1) "I lost my bank card, so I can't take out money right now"
2) "I get paid next week, is it okay if I hit you up then?"
3) "I was on my way out the door, and I left the money on my counter. Damn! I promise I'll have it for you next week".

Isn't it funny that he's always got money for a beer after the game?...

Player's skill level: 8
Player's likeability in the dressing room: 7 (3 if you're the Captain)

"The Celebrator"

"He shoots, he scores! The Hawks win! The Hawks win!"

"The Celebrator" is the Beer League player that goes completely overboard when something goes well for his team (particularly him scoring a goal!)

You'd think that this guy just won the lottery!

"The Celebrator" really needs to be careful on the ice because of his extremely irritating attitude towards his opposition. (See "The Goon" - pg. 24). I mean hey, everybody likes to score a goal or win a hockey game, but come on now, it's not the seventh game of the Stanley Cup Finals, bud!

As a teammate, you love this player's enthusiasm, although it can get to the point where it just becomes embarrassing.

"Hey Bobby, we're up 9-0 - relax!"

From fist pumps to throwing gloves - "The Celebrator" brings something new to the table each and every week...

...now stop riding your stick - you're making your team look bad!

Player's skill level: 6
Player's likeability in the dressing room: 4

"The Escape Artist"

"Hey buddy, how'd you get out of the house tonight?"

Players will bug this guy any opportunity they get. "The Escape Artist" is the guy that "needs permission" to go out and play his game.

This player in on a tight leash. All he wants is a night out with the boys, and that's not an easy task. "The Escape Artist" really needs to sweet talk his way into getting out of the house.

"Baby, I'll bring home dinner tomorrow night after work if you'd like!"

Hey, whatever it takes to make it on time for puck drop.

"The Escape Artist" is an average player on the roster, although his main focus is to get the game over with as quick as possible, so he can go out and have a beer afterwards. This is his one day a week that he's allowed out of the house, so he might as well make the most of it.

Now when a second ice time in one week becomes available, that's when "The Escape Artist" has to be *really* crafty. He'll actually call a buddy to pick him up so his wife doesn't hear him starting the car, and he'll creep out for an hour in hopes that she doesn't notice. Sometimes a great idea, but if she catches him in the act - look out! "No hockey for one month!"

If he's not there to help out the team, you know "The Escape Artist" is there in spirit. Too bad he got stuck doing the dishes.

Player's skill level: 6
Player's likeability in the dressing room: 8

"The Chick"

Every now and then you'll be skating around in warm-up and have a quick glance over at the other team. There's one player you notice that has a long ponytail hanging out of the back of their helmet. You're reaction is: "Is that a girl?"

This particular player is known as "The Chick".

Occasionally, a female will sign up for a "Men's League". Now there could be a number of reasons why she wanted to play with the men over a Women's League. And guys around the league will do anything and everything as to find out why!

She's heard every cheesy line like - "You're too cute to be playing in this league".

Watch "The Chick" play, and you'll quickly discover that she's quite a good player out there. Some players will be offended by this, while others are mesmerized. It's a little known fact that most Beer Leaguer's love girls that play hockey.

"It's like combining my two favourite things".

She's popular on and off the ice, look out for "The Chick" in a Beer League near you.

Player's skill level: 7
Player's likeability in the dressing room: N/A...?

"The Puck-Hog"

If you're looking for someone to play with that will give you a nice pass, then keep this guy off your line. This of course is "The Puck-Hog".

This guy is one of the most common Beer League players that you will ever find hanging around a hockey rink. "The Puck-Hog" is the player that hangs on to the puck *way* too long without ever distributing it to his teammates. Opponents will chase him around the ice trying to steal the puck off him as he skates around in circles with no regard for the other four players on his team.

He's generally a pretty decent stick-handler, but that doesn't matter if he's a one-man show out there. This player is responsible for the phrase: *There's no "I" in team.*

Sometimes "The Puck-Hog" doesn't want to pass the puck because he has very little confidence in the rest of his teammates. He'll dangle around his opposition and take the shot himself. Most cases however, he's just looking to be the "superstar" of the team. He's a selfish player, although he has been known to pot quite a few goals.

Talk to "The Stat-Tracker" (see pg. 42) and he'll show you this player's Beer League statistics:
20 games, 25 goals, 1 assist (his shot bounced off his teammates head and into the net), 26 points, and 13 angry teammates.

Player's skill level: 8
Player's likeability in the dressing room: 2

"The Ice-Hog"

Not to be confused with "The Puck-Hog" (see previous page), "The Ice-Hog" is his brother who over-stays his welcome on every shift.

It's Beer League Hockey. Everyone pays to play, so the ice time should be divided evenly with the players, right? Not according to this guy.

"The Ice-Hog" is oblivious to the fact that there are other players on his bench. He will double and triple shift while his linemates sit impatiently.

"Get off the ice!" will often be shouted from his bench once he's on for his third-straight minute. Teams need a whistle in order to ever get this guy off, and even then it'll take a tap on the shoulder.

"Hey bud – there are other players on the team, you know?"

Like his brother, he's usually a pretty good player hence the reason he legs so much ice time. But when he's one of the weaker players – look out. "The Ice-Hog" has been known to get the boot from a team before the season is half over.

Player's skill level: 7
Player's likeability in the dressing room: 2

"The Borrower"

"Hey man, can I borrow some tape?"

What's that? You want to *borrow* someone's tape? How exactly does that work anyways - were you planning on giving it back after the game?

"The Borrower" is the player that is always looking to borrow something, and will rummage through his teammate's bags until he finds what he's looking for.

Anyone else would call it stealing. With this guy - nah, he's just borrowing.

What "The Borrower" doesn't understand is that a roll of stick tape, stick wax, shin-pad tape, a six-pack - they all cost money! And yes, over the course of the season, this mooch manages to get it all for free.

"Dude, get your own stuff!"

"The Borrower" might be annoying, but good luck finding a team without one.

Player's skill level: 5
Player's likeability in the dressing room: 3

"Meet Me Outside"

As alluded to in the first chapter of this book, the great thing about the game of Beer League Hockey is players can always leave their differences on the ice.

OK, well there's always an exception to every rule.

"Meet Me Outside" has a whole different mentality, and doesn't know when to just *let it go*. The minute a referee or opposing player gets under his skin, this guy flips like there's no tomorrow. The minute he's removed from a game, the conversation turns into where exactly the fight is going down *after* the game.

"I'll see you outside @%#hole! I'll be in the parking lot!"

The problem with this player is that once he gets going, there's no stopping him. When expressing his interest of *getting together after the game*, his opposition will let him have it, fueling the situation even further.

This guy is a ticking time bomb waiting to go off. Not much of a skilled player, "Meet Me Outside" is more interested in getting into a big bout then actually playing the game. Look out when he and "The Goon" (see pg. 24) meet up. Fireworks are bound to happen!...Just try and stay away from the cars, would ya?

Player's skill level: 3
Player's likeability in the dressing room: 3

"The Cherry-Picker"

Don't ever expect to see this player inside your own blueline. He's too busy hanging around centre ice looking for a pass. That of course is "The Cherry-Picker".

Cherry-picking is a tactic in sports in which a player hangs out behind his defence in hopes of receiving an open pass and eventually scoring. In other words, this player does nothing to help his team out, other than waiting for a pass to send him in all alone.

If it wasn't for offsides, this guy would be camping out in front of his opposing team's goalie!

"The Cherry-Picker" is a lazy player that is afraid to get his nose dirty. There's no grit or determination from him - and it drives his teammates nuts. If the opposing team has the puck, essentially they're on the power play because he's nowhere to be seen. Players on his bench will yell at him to join the play, but he's extremely stubborn and will pretend not to hear them.

Can he put the puck in the net? For the most part, yes he can. But who can't score goals if every single one of them is on a breakaway?

If his team had a coach, (see "The Scotty Bowman - pg. 20), this guy would be benched! "The Cherry-Picker" hurts his team more than he helps it.

Player's skill level: 4
Player's likeability in the dressing room: 4

"The Trainer"

Believe it or not, from time to time Beer League teams will carry this individual over the course of a season. Not an actual player on a roster, but an asset to the team, he's none other than "The Trainer".

"The Trainer" is the guy who never really played much hockey growing up. But on the other hand, he's one of the biggest fans of the game.

He's there to help out anyone. He'll fill up your water bottles, tape up your stick, and will even throw in some insight over the course of the game. He has even been known to bring his old *ghettoblaster* to the room for some pre-game tunes.

Did somebody say "Eye of the Tiger?"

Other teams find it comical that a Beer League team would carry "The Trainer", although his teammates cherish him. When asking him about opposing teams talking smack about him, his response is: "They're just jealous!"

A solid guy to have in the dressing room, "The Trainer" is always there to support his team.

Player's skill level: N/A
Player's likeability in the dressing room: 8

"The Diver"

Get a couple of feet next to this guy, and he'll be down on the ice like a sack of potatoes. He's one of Beer League's peskiest players known as "The Diver".

Diving (also referred to as embellishment) is a term used to describe the way a player tries to get the attention of the referee by embellishing an infraction from an opposing player in an attempt to draw a penalty.

His drama teacher would be proud.

"The Diver" flops around during a game, aggravating his opponents on a nightly basis. He will be verbally attacked for three periods, but always sticks to his game plan. Does it work? In many cases, yes, in which teams will lose their minds. But when it doesn't work, this player will just look foolish.

Now "The Diver's" tactics can also come back to haunt him if the referee throws him in the box for "two minutes for diving". It's the sweetest revenge an opposing Beer League team can receive, especially if they put one past his goalie on the ensuing power-play.

This Beer League player gets a perfect score of 10...for the dive. Now throw a gold medal around his neck - he deserved it!

Player's skill level: 4
Player's likeability in the dressing room: 4

"Mr. Superstitious"

"I've scored in six straight games wearing this shirt! I can't wash it now!"

Of course! It's the moldy shirt that you're wearing as to why you're playing so well. This is Beer League's "Mr. Superstitious".

The game of hockey and superstitious behaviour have gone hand in hand for years. "Mr. Superstitious", however steps it up a notch. When it's game day, he'll actually go through different pre-game rituals expecting that they will have some sort of bearing on how he's going to play.

This trend will normally take place regarding extremely positive or extremely negative aspects of this player's game. Score a hat-trick, then stick to what you're doing. Don't score a goal in five games, change everything up. That is the mentality of "Mr. Superstitious".

As a player, he's usually a pretty good one. He's a streaky guy that will score you points. He has also been known to pass some of his traits on to the rest of the dressing room.

From playoff beards (see "The Stache" - pg. 71) to un-washed jock straps, "Mr. Superstitious" will always provide the team with fresh new rituals.

Player's skill level: 6
Player's likeability in the dressing room: 7

"The Angry Goalie"

Easy big fella! It's not the end of the world, you just let a puck go by you. This belligerent character is known as "The Angry Goalie".

What's funny about "The Angry Goalie" is that every goal he's ever let in is somebody else's fault, or he has to give a reason as to why he got scored on. Buddy, it's just a goal, get over it!

"The Angry Goalie" is commonly known for smashing his stick and cursing at his teammates!

"Get the &$@# outta my way, you're screening me!"

The problem with "The Angry Goalie" is he brings his whole team down. With all of the bickering you're hearing behind you, it's hard to want to back this guy up. If you're playing up to his standards, he'll keep his mouth shut. But one bad pass up the centre of the ice, (see "Mr. Giveaway - pg. 74), and he'll tear you a new one!

He's a passionate player, which actually makes him a decent goalie. But teams know that if they get a couple past him early, then they're laughing the rest of the way as he's completely thrown off his game.

A nice guy off the ice, but a nut case on the ice, "The Angry Goalie" can be found in almost every Beer League. Just make sure to wear a back brace if you plan on standing in front of him.

Player's skill level: 5
Player's likeability in the dressing room: 3

"The Big Guy"

Standing in at 6' 5" and weighing in at 325 pounds, he's Beer League Hockey's - "The Big Guy".

"The Big Guy" makes guys who are typically above average in size, look like pip-squeaks. He's one of the most intimidating players that you will ever run into on the ice...

...just make sure you don't run into him.

Players are surprised to see that "The Big Guy" can actually skate for being so huge. And good luck getting around him. He's your most solid defenceman and will throw players around like a rag-doll especially if they're standing in his goalie's crease.

Now for the most part, "The Big Guy" can also be referred to as "The Friendly Giant", but that is until you make him mad. Fire this guy up, and you'll wish you hadn't. This monster will take out the trash with just about anybody in the league, and will even give "The Goon" (see pg. 24) a good run for his money.

The only knock on "The Big Guy" is his cardio. Give him one or two rushes up and down the ice, and he's ready for a line-change. Hey, no big deal - he did his job!

He's a must for any roster looking to add the "intimidating factor" to their team. Look out for "The Big Guy" at an arena near you!

Player's skill level: 6
Player's likeability in the dressing room: 9

"The Follower"

"Hello! Anybody home?!"

This guy can not take the hint! "The Follower" is the player (formerly on a Beer League team) that never got invited back to play with the team the next season. Oddly enough, he still shows up anyways.

It gets worse. If and when "The Follower" gets booted by the team, he'll still pop by the rink from time to time to watch his former team play. What is he waiting for an injury or something?

Now there are many reasons as to why a team doesn't invite "The Follower" back. Aside from the fact that he's an awful player, this guy just does not fit in right with the dressing room. Ever hear of the term "Awkward?!" Well, that was originated from a conversation with this guy. Players in the dressing room can be sharing a great story, and once this guy pipes up, all you hear are crickets.

"The Follower" means well, but no really cares. Although he can be quite the sneaky individual, as more often than not, he somehow manages to squeak himself back on to the team.

Captains beware! Do not give this guy your cell phone number! He will call and beg you until you're forced to give in. (He may even add you to his speed dial). Look out for this guy - once he's brought in, he's next to impossible to let go!

Player's skill level: 3
Player's likeability in the dressing room: 1

"The Spaz"

OK, so there are players out there that like to flip out at the officials (see "The Angry Guy - pg. 39) and then there are players who take things *way* too seriously (see "Mr. Serious" - pg. 34). Well this player is on a whole other level. "The Spaz" is the Beer League player that flips out on his *own* teammates!

"Dude, I thought we were all friends here?"

Evidently you're not.

This guy will pull things out of his hat that you thought you'd never see or hear in a game of Beer League Hockey. From throwing water bottles at his defenceman, to actually trying to fight one of his linemates for not passing him the puck, this drama queen will frustrate your entire squad to no end.

It's actually very strange, because off the ice, he's one of the nicest guys you'll ever encounter. But once he throws on a pair of skates, it's like flipping on a different switch. His teammates have a real difficult time of dealing with him night in and night out.

Typically, "The Spaz" doesn't last a full season with his team. Once players realize just how much of a nut-job he is, "The Organizer" (see pg. 28) politely informs him that his services are no longer required. He just better make sure he cuts him over the phone or a line-brawl might ensue!

Player's skill level: 3
Player's likeability in the dressing room: 1

"The Naked Guy"

There's always a lot of chatter in the dressing room after a hard-fought Beer League hockey game. But for some reason, this player prefers to *disrobe* before joining in on the chatter. This of course is "The Naked Guy".

"Hey man, that's a great story, but can you please put some clothes on!"

No one really knows why "The Naked Guy" enjoys being naked so much. He's so comfortable being in the nude, you'd think he had all of his clothes on when he's talking to you. It's one thing to be sitting down with your gear off after the game with a towel around you, but this guy walks around telling stories like nothing's the matter.

Put him on a team with "Mr. Uncomfortable" (see pg. 27) and that's a recipe for disaster!

At times, one would suggest that the only reason he's on the team is to hang out in the showers afterwards....weird. Others will tell you that he's just doing it for a laugh.

On the ice, "The Naked Guy" is actually a great player. He's played a lot of hockey over the years and is usually one of the more experienced players on the team. (At least he's covered up out there!)

"The Naked Guy" is one of the better guys to have on your team, just make sure you keep your head up when talking to him.

Player's skill level: 7
Player's likeability in the dressing room: 7 (1 if you're "Mr. Uncomfortable")

"The Chirper"

"What are you gonna do about it, buddy? Huh? You wanna go? Bring it on, pal!"

Throw a few expletives in there, and that's typically the type of conversation that you'll get out of Beer League's most hated player - "The Chirper".

Anybody that plays Beer League Hockey knows that there will be some chatter on the ice from time to time. It's a physical sport with grown men that all have a level of competitiveness inside of them. Nevertheless, "The Chirper" takes it to a whole other level as he runs his mouth on every shift.

The puzzling thing about this guy is he's typically one of the puniest guys on the ice. So why the big mouth little man? "The Chirper" infuriates teams (particularly "The Goon" - see pg. 24) to the point that they want to physically destroy him.

The most frustrating thing about "The Chirper" is he's actually one of the better players on a Beer League roster. The reason he's running his mouth is because he just scored two goals on you, or he put the puck through your legs on his last rush.

Hey, what's a Beer League without a little trash talk, right? Just be prepared to back it up!

Player's skill level: 7
Player's likeability in the dressing room: 5

"The Lazy Guy"

He's the one guy that drives his teammates absolutely bonkers on a nightly basis. "The Lazy Guy" is the player who has no desire to move his feet...or do anything for that matter.

It's mind-boggling that a player will even sign-up to play hockey and then literally do nothing every time he steps on the ice.

His lazy habits include:

1) No back-checking
2) One-hand on the stick
3) Standing around watching the play

This guy will drive "The Scotty Bowman" nuts! (See pg. 20). There are 12 other guys on the bench that would love to be out there contributing, but "The Lazy Guy" just won't give them a chance.

So why do teams continue to carry this guy? Either his dad paid for the team jerseys, or he generously covers the tab after the game.

A true pain to have on any Beer League roster, "The Lazy Guy" will definitely put you to sleep.

Player's skill level: 2
Player's likeability in the dressing room: 2

"Mr. Sportsmanship"

"Put 'er there, pal. You played a helluva game".

He is the Beer League player that gives the utmost respect to every player he steps on the ice with. A true gentleman both on and off the ice, "Mr. Sportsmanship" is the squeakiest clean player you will ever play with.

When accidentally knocking an opponent down to the ice you'll hear a sincere "Sorry about that" behind the play. If a player drops his stick, he'll be the first guy to pick it up and hand it back to him. He'll even compliment his opposition for scoring a nice goal.

"Mr. Sportsmanship" is just happy to be out for a skate each week. He understands that it's just a game, and it's all about having fun. As a player, he's actually pretty talented. His "think pass before shoot" mentality creates a ton of scoring chances for his linemates every week. He will often lead the league in assists, (just ask "The Stat-Tracker - pg. 42) and he'll never hit the sin-bin once over the course of the season.

Even "The Goon" (see pg. 24) will leave this guy alone. "Mr. Sportsmanship" has built up such a rapport with the league that he brings out the best in everyone.

But hey, when you're losing 9-1 – stop high-fiving the other team would ya?

Player's skill level: 7
Player's likeability in the dressing room: 9

"The Instigator"

He will poke and prod at you every time you play against him. "The Instigator" is the dirtiest player on a team and is always looking to cause problems.

As soon as the referee turns his back on him, "The Instigator" will sweep a guy off his feet and pretend like nothing happened.

"Huh? What did I do?"

Poll a league of 100 players, and 99 of them will tell you that this player is the most hated guy in the league. His sole purpose of playing is to get under people's skin. And boy is he good at it. Many will compare "The Instigator" to "The Chirper" (see pg. 67), however there is a very distinct difference. "The Chirper" will just run his mouth, while "The Instigator" will actually try to hurt his opponents.

Is he a good guy to have on your team? Some would say yes. Although carrying a player like this on your roster can result in a league full of teams hating you because of him.

He's made the expression "There's always *one* on every team" famous. Keep your head up when you're on the ice with "The Instigator". He's out to make your life a living hell...

Player's skill level: 5
Player's likeability in the dressing room: 4

"The Stache"

Who said that the 70's look is out of style? "The Stache" is the Beer League Player who sports a classic moustache to show off to his peers. There are many different shapes and styles that players will work on, but they never disappoint.

You'll often find "The Stache" sporting huge chops as well. (These help compliment the moustache).

Many professional hockey players have brought back this look, and the idea has seemingly been picked up by Beer League players across the world.

"The Stache" is also a very popular player come playoff time. Once the post-season arrives, players start to grow the "playoff beard" (an old superstition that has been a part of hockey for years) in which they are not allowed to shave until the end of their season. At times, players that usually provide a clean-shaven look, decide to grow a perfect stache rather than the "playoff beard", in which much grooming is involved.

It's a great look, as at times it can intimidate your opponents. "The Stache" is one of the veterans on the team and a solid all-around player. He's cocky but can back it up. A true "womanizer" off the ice, and a force to be reckoned with on the ice, "The Stache" is an asset to any Beer League roster.

Player's skill level: 8
Player's likeability in the dressing room: 9

"The Shot-Blocker"

OK, so it's a 6-2 game, and there's three minutes left on the clock. The biggest guy on the opposing team is teeing up his cannon of a shot from the blueline, and what does this guy do? He lays down in front of it.

Meet "The Shot-Blocker".

Teammates will appreciate the efforts made by this player, although they all know he's not very smart. Doesn't he realize that it's Beer League Hockey, and getting a fractured rib or a broken nose isn't worth it? Good luck changing his mind about it.

"The Shot-Blocker" isn't a very good player, but he does have heart. Since he can't put the puck in the net, (or do anything worthwhile with the puck for that matter), laying down in front of shots is the easiest way for this guy to be the hero without having to do too much. To him, feeling that *thud* hit him in the chest is better then dangling the twine.

His teammates will always congratulate him for his heroics (for better lack of terms). "The Shot-Blocker" is actually a pretty good guy to throw into a game when there's a faceoff in his team's zone. In fact, this guy hopes that his team *loses* the draw, just so he can skate out to the point and do what he does best!

"*Sweet*! This one's gonna hurt!"

Player's skill level: 3
Player's likeability in the dressing room: 7

"The Recruiter"

This guy will hang around the rink keeping his eyes open for any new talent that he could draw to his Beer League team. Often the *co-captain* of his squad, "The Recruiter" is the player that looks to steal players from their current team to join his.

"The Recruiter" also shows up to arenas that he doesn't typically play in so he can take a look at other talent not currently seen in his Beer League. Once he spots a player that might make a good fit for his team, he's all over it.

"Hey man - you interested in playing *twice* a week? We've got a team that could really use an extra player!"

He's a pretty convincing guy, and will always deliver a great sales pitch as to "why" you would want to play on his team.

"The Recruiter" also loves to show up to "shinny" or pick-up hockey as there are plenty of good players kicking around the rink that don't currently play on any Beer League teams. "The Recruiter" has actually been known to swindle deals with players with such incentives as a "free jersey" or "play for 1/2 price" in order to get these guys on his squad.

What's next for this guy - tryout camps? Oops, hopefully that just didn't give him any ideas...

Player's skill level: 5
Player's likeability in the dressing room: 5

"Mr. Giveaway"

This poor guy just can't catch a break. He's the player that loves to turn the puck over to the other team in the worst of situations. He's none other then "Mr. Giveaway".

Now hey, we all make mistakes from time to time, but this guy is relentless. His turnovers could never come at a worse time, and his teammates love to razz him for it.

It's a 3-2 game with 30 seconds left....ya, you best keep this guy on the bench.

His teammates will often question him if he's colour-blind by the way he *gift wraps* the puck and hands it over to his opponents.

"What team are you playing for, anyways?"

He's really not a bad player, he just loves to crack under pressure. "Mr. Giveaway" will get quite a few points over the season, which is why the team keeps him on the roster. If only he could receive an assist on his opponent's goals, you'd be looking at the league's point leader!

"Mr. Giveaway" is also quite popular for blowing a shutout for his team, just ask "The Wall" (see pg. 47). Fortunately for him, it's Beer League and he doesn't need to worry about getting benched!

Often the opposition's best friend, "Mr. Giveaway" is always good for a few laughs!

Player's skill level: 6
Player's likeability in the dressing room: 7

"The Bobby Orr"

"Don't worry guys - I've got this one!"

He's the defenceman on your team that likes to take the puck "coast to coast". Meet "The Bobby Orr".

Now as any true hockey fan will tell you, the *real* Bobby Orr was one of the greatest defenceman in the history of the game. On countless occasions, Mr. Orr would take the puck from one end of the ice to the other, weaving his way in and out of his opponents, and pocketing the puck in the back of the net.

That's not the case with this guy!

Once "The Bobby Orr" sees a bit of daylight, he will take the puck and barrel up the ice with his head down hoping for a highlight-reel goal. Unfortunately for him and his teammates, it usually ends up in a turnover to the opposing team. His forwards will curse him each and every time he attempts this as they are often stuck standing at the blueline or forced offside.

Hey pal, ever heard of "head-manning the puck?"

People will often confuse him with "The Puck-Hog" (see pg. 54), however they're actually quite different players. While "The Puck-Hog" has some pretty good puck-handling abilities, "The Bobby Orr" just forgets that he has teammates!

His ridiculous end-to-end rushes usually work out for him once every 30 tries, but when it happens, he's a pretty happy guy. "Wow, it finally worked!" Too bad no one else on his team is impressed.

If teams were smart they'd just throw this guy on forward.

Player's skill level: 4
Player's likeability in the dressing room: 3

"The Mama's Boy"

"Mom - look! The nice referee gave me the game puck for scoring a goal!"

He's 40 years old, and his mom still comes to watch him play. Simply put, he's "The Mama's Boy".

The troubling thing about this player is it's not just a few games that his mom comes out to watch. It's every game of the season! In fact, the "Mama's Boy" actually gets his mom to drive him to each game because he doesn't have a driver's license.

"Why drive if Mama can drive me?"

"The Mama's Boy" is one of the worst players on your team and is often compared to "The Pylon". (See pg. 46).

During the course of the game, you'll see them wave to each other between whistles, and smile over certain plays. If "The Mama's Boy" gets knocked to the ice, his mom's shoe will instantly be removed as she bangs it on the glass in disapproval.

When made fun of for having his mom still take him to hockey, he simply answers "Wouldn't you like free ice-cream on the way home from hockey?"

I guess he has a point there.

Player's skill level: 2
Player's likeability in the dressing room: 3

"The Veteran"

He's 42 years old but has the legs of a 19 year old. "The Veteran" is one of the League's most beloved players who have been playing the sport of Beer League Hockey for decades.

Players love "The Veteran" as he always brings something to the table. Generally he's the smartest player on the team. He has incredible hockey sense, and is rock solid on defence. He may not have the same scoring touch that he did 20 years ago, but he will still find ways to put the puck in the back of the net.

What's also great about the "Veteran" is he fits in well with the dressing room. He's always good for a new story, and he really knows how to get his team fired up before a big game.

"The Veteran" will always stick up for his teammates. If he sees one of his players in trouble, he won't be afraid to skate over and drop the mitts if necessary.

A Beer League team isn't complete without him. "The Veteran" is a must for any Beer League club looking to take home the title.

Player's skill level: 7
Player's likeability in the dressing room: 10

"The Rental Goalie"

"Come on, come on, ring already!"

He sits patiently each night waiting for a phone call from one of the League Captains (see "The Organizer pg. 28). Meet "The Rental Goalie".

This guy is without a doubt the most popular player in the sport of Beer League Hockey. "The Rental Goalie" is the tender that can never land a full time team to play with, but instead is the call-up goalie that teams use when their regular goalie can't make it. Like "The Die-Hard" (see pg. 37), "The Rental Goalie" is always itching to play. In fact, this goalie receives more games in a season than most full time goalies.

The best thing about "The Rental Goalie" is his reliability. If a team finds out that their goalie can't make it 10 minutes before game time, it's a quick call over to this guy, and problem solved!

Skill wise, he's actually a very good goalie. Playing four to five times a week continues to make him stronger and stronger every season.

A great guy to keep on speed dial, "The Rental Goalie" will always be there for his fellow Beer Leaguer's.

Player's skill level: 7
Player's likeability in the dressing room: 7

"The Legend"

He's the player that everyone in the dressing room wants to be like. Funny that it has nothing to do with hockey.

Not popular because of his on-ice play, "The Legend" proves himself off the ice and in the dressing room with his, well, exceptionally large anatomy.

It takes a while for someone to actually mention "The Legend's" so-called "gift". In fact, sometimes it's never mentioned at all. Usually conversations about "The Legend" will begin outside the dressing room after a few beers with:

"Did you see the size of buddy's - ?!"

The fact of the matter is, everyone on his Beer League team knows it, whether it's been talked about or not. (Even "Mr. Uncomfortable" - see pg. 27).

The great thing about "The Legend" is that once the cat is out of the bag, the jokes never stop. Does it butter him up? Yeah sure, why wouldn't he? It's what keeps this guy coming back to the team each season!

A classic character to have on your team, "The Legend" will live on forever...

Player's skill level: 7
Player's likeability in the dressing room: 8

"The Stud"

He's the one guy that *everyone* in the league wants on their team. He's the ever-popular Beer League player known as "The Stud".

The interesting thing about "The Stud" is he has never played any professional hockey. He's simply the guy that's been playing Beer League Hockey before he was old enough to walk into a bar.

When it comes to Beer Leagues, he is simply the best. If you show up to the rink and you know you're playing "The Stud's" team, you might as well pack it in and go home.

"The Stud" is so good, that it's been told that teammates will usually let him play for free and chip in the extra cost themselves!

"The Recruiter" (see pg. 73) and "Mr. Serious" (see pg. 34) are always looking to recruit this guy for upcoming seasons. And why not? "The Stud" leads the league in points each and every season.

"The Stud" also looks out for his team in the toughness department. If one of his teammates are getting picked on, he's the first one there to back him up. (That is unless "The Goon" (see pg. 24) got a hold of him first). He's you're all-around player that will never let you down, and that's why teammates love him.

The true great in ice rinks worldwide - "The Stud" is the all-time Beer League icon.

Player's skill level: 10
Player's likeability in the dressing room: 10

CHAPTER 3

The Men in Stripes

**They're the guys you love to hate,
but what's a hockey game without them?**

The Men in Stripes

1) "Mr. Cranky" 85
2) "The Old-Timer Pt. 2" 86
3) "The Drunk Guy Pt. 2" 87
4) "The Agitator" 88
5) "Clueless" 89
6) "Mr. Officer" 90

Why show up to the rink if you don't want to be there? "Mr. Cranky" is a perfect example of this.

The moment he steps on the ice, opposing teams groan as if to say "Not this guy, again!" And they have a good point. "Mr. Cranky" would rather be anywhere than at the hockey rink.

The problem with this official is he has seen so many hockey games that it's just not fun for him anymore. He has dealt with so many profanities directed at him over the years, that his self-confidence is destroyed, and the sight of hockey just makes him angry.

So why does he stick around? He just can't seem to let it go. Deep down, "Mr. Cranky" loves getting in on the action every night. Players might get him riled up, but at the end of the day, he wouldn't know what to do with himself without making trips to the arena each week.

Players typically can't stand "Mr. Cranky" as he's the guy that calls a ton of penalties. (Often soft calls). But say one word to him, and he'll quickly be telling you to *hit the showers*.

There's not a Beer League in the world that doesn't have this guy in the rotation. Keep your stick on the ice and your mouth zipped shut. That will make for a much better experience for everyone.

Amount of refereed games per week: 20-24
Likeability throughout the league: 2

"The Old-Timer Pt. 2"

"Stop it! Please stop fighting! Why is no one listening to me?"

"The Old Guy Pt. 2" is the veteran official who has been refereeing hockey games for over 50 years. If asked, he could recite the entire rule book to you from start to finish.

This guy has seen every possible event take place in Beer League Hockey from bench clearing brawls to glass shattering body checks, to games with final scores of 20-19. Nothing will ever surprise this official.

"The Old Guy Pt. 2" is still a great ref, but at times he simply can't keep up with the play. Players will yell at him if he misses a call (he can barely see), but once they realize who it is, they just improvise.

"It's the Old Guy - what do you expect?"

Players really like "The Old Guy Pt. 2" because he is harmless and means well when he's on the ice. He shows no bias towards teams, and he's pretty easy to get a long with. He's one of Beer League's all-time greats...just go easy on him out there, would ya?

Amount of refereed games per week: 16-20
Likeability throughout the league: 8

"The Drunk Guy Pt. 2"

Who ever said that there's no drinking on the job? "The Drunk Guy Pt. 2" will tell you that's just a myth.

It's pretty obvious to Beer League teams that when this guy is officiating, he's half in the bag...sometimes completely. Players will line up to take a face-off and it smells like a liquor cabinet. They'll take a peek up, and notice that his eyes are half closed while sporting a goofy smile on his face.

"Let'shavesomefunouttherboys!"

"The Drunk Guy Pt. 2" is clearly a mess. He shows up to the rink with a couple in him, but after his third or fourth game, he's usually polished off a case. His performance will slowly dwindle between each game, and it's quite noticeable the later you play that night.

You know a guy is wrecked if he's using the boards to keep himself up.

"The Drunk Guy Pt. 2" will miss almost every call. He's completely in la-la-land from the opening puck drop. His biggest problem is chirping to the other teams on every mistake *they* make. This official has been known to laugh up a storm when a player falls down, or a goalie let's in a soft one.

Not a smart move when you're dealing with 25 Beer League players! This guy will take a verbal beating on a nightly basis, and rightfully so!

Amount of refereed games per week: 8-10
Likeability throughout the league: 2

"The Agitator"

"Say another word and I'll kick you out. Come on - I dare you, ya big jerk - say something!"

He's Beer League's most hated referee - "The Agitator".

This cocky official has been gracing Beer Leagues for years, and really knows how to get under a player's skin. From the moment the puck is dropped he's keeping a close eye on everyone, eagerly awaiting a chance to call his first penalty.

"The Agitator" has the memory of an elephant. He never forgets a face, even if he hasn't officiated them in years. He's also very good at remembering players numbers for future reference.

"Hmm, that's the guy that called me an $&%hole!"

That's right. Don't ever get in this guy's doghouse, or you'll be sure to regret it. "The Agitator" is known for goading players on. If they don't like his penalty call, he'll try and sucker them into taking another one. This drives players nuts, and he will feed off this.

Known for his famous "2, 10, and the game", "The Agitator" will make player's lives miserable!

Amount of refereed games per week: 12-15
Likeability throughout the league: 1

"Clueless"

You almost have to feel sorry for this guy. "Clueless" is the referee that really doesn't know the rules of Beer League Hockey.

His problem is that players can sense that he looks uncomfortable and vulnerable the first time they see him. He gives off an *I don't know what I'm doing* appearance every time he hits the ice.

"Clueless" is known for his late whistles and missed offside calls. Players really get on this guy when he doesn't know a certain ruling on a play. (Thank God he has a partner out there). Once he makes a bad penalty call, players will be all over him! (Particularly "The Angry Guy" - see pg. 39). The problem is, "Clueless" is too nice of a guy to ever kick anyone out a game. Well, either that or he's too scared to.

Now occasionally players will give this guy a break, as many times "Clueless" is one of the newer referees on the squad.

"Come on fellas, cut this guy some slack!"

While other times, teams will just unleash on him. Let's face it, there are 25 other "referees" on the benches each game as it is, so when you've got a guy that really doesn't know the rules out there, you know there's bound to be problems!

Not with a lack of trying, "Clueless" will give it his all each and every night. Just keep your fingers crossed that he calls in sick.

Amount of refereed games per week: 4-6
Like-ability throughout the league: 2

"Mr. Officer"

As a Beer League player, whatever you do, don't cross the path of "Mr. Officer". This guy means business.

Everyone appreciates a guy that takes his job seriously. But then there's "Mr. Officer". Quite frankly, he goes way over-board when officiating a Beer League game. This guy doesn't take a word from anyone or else they're in trouble! Not to mention he's not afraid of throwing you out of the game...literally!

This official is on a permanent power trip. You will never get him to crack a smile, and no chance will you ever get in his good books. "Mr. Officer" is there to police teams until the final buzzer sounds.

So why such a stern approach? One might suggest that "Mr. Officer" wishes that he were an actual police officer. Refereeing Beer Leagues is his only way of getting to push people around and put them in their place.

This referee also thrives when a fight breaks out. It's his one chance to truly get his hands dirty. "Mr. Officer" will come in and break up a fight as he inflicts more punishment on the combatants than they did to themselves. He'll boot the players out the rink door as if he were throwing them into the slammer.

"Ah, one less criminal to get off the ice!"

Amount of refereed games per week: 16-20
Like-ability throughout the league: 4

CHAPTER 4

Terms From the Dressing Room

A guide to better understanding hockey dressing room jargon

Terms From the Dressing Room

Barn: Another word for a hockey arena. Funny that there are many Beer League rinks around the world that actually look like a barn. That's what makes them so vintage for Beer League Hockey.
    Example: "The team packed up their bags and headed to the *barn*".
    Beer League Characters best represented: All
    Classic Beer League expression regarding this term: "I love this *barn*!"

Beauty: This hockey term has two different meanings: A) A nice play on the ice, particularly a great goal. B) A player who is a real character on the team.
    Example: A) "He deked his opponent and scored a *beauty*" B) "Larry is a real *beauty*"
    Beer League Characters best represented: A) "The Stud" (pg. 80), B) "Mr. Cooperalls" (pg. 17)
    Classic Beer League expression regarding this term: A) "That was a *beauty* goal!" B) "He's a *beauty*!"

Biscuit: Another term for a puck.
    Example: "The *biscuit* was shot over the boards and out of play".
    Beer League Characters best represented: All
    Classic Beer League expression regarding this term: "Shoot the *biscuit*!"

Blowing a tire: A term used to describe a player tripping and falling to the ice for no apparent reason.
    Example: "As the player tried to turn, he *blew a tire* and went into the boards".
    Beer League Characters best represented: "The Pylon" (pg. 46), "The Drunk Guy" (pg. 48)
    Classic Beer League expression regarding this term: "Learn how to skate!"

Bread Basket: A shot taken in a players mid-section, particularly the goalie.
    Example: "The goalie stopped the puck right in the *bread basket*".
    Beer League Characters best represented: "The Wall" (pg. 47), "The Shot-Blocker" (pg. 72)
    Classic Beer League expression regarding this term: "How's your *bread basket*?"

Bucket: Another term used for a hockey helmet.
    Example: "Andy got hit so hard that his *bucket* flew off".
    Beer League Characters best represented: "The Klima" (pg. 31)
    Classic Beer League expression regarding this term: N/A

Chicklets: Another word for a player's teeth.
    Example: "That high stick to the face knocked the player's *chicklets* out".
    Beer League Characters best represented: "Mr. Glass" (pg. 49), "The Goon" (pg. 24)
    Classic Beer League expression regarding this term: "Pick up your *chicklets*!"

Clapper: Another word used to describe a slapshot. Generally a "clapper" is taken from the point by a defenceman.
    Example: "The goalie stopped a tough *clapper* late in the game".
    Beer League Characters best represented: "The Big Guy" (pg. 63), "The Head-Hunter" (pg. 15)
    Classic Beer League expression regarding this term: "Nice *clapper*!"

Coast-to-Coast: Describes a player taking the puck themselves from one end of the ice and down to the other.
    Example: "Look at that player go *coast-to-coast*!"
    Beer League Characters best represented: "The Puck-Hog" (pg. 54), "The Bobby Orr" (pg. 75)
    Classic Beer League expression regarding this term: "There are other players out there!

Dance: When two players are ready to fight, this can be referred to as a "dance". Often Beer League fights result in two players just spinning around with no real punches being thrown.
    Example: "The gloves are off, and these two are about to *dance*!"
    Beer League Characters best represented: "The Big Guy" (pg. 63), "The Goon" (pg. 24)
    Classic Beer League expression regarding this term: "You wanna *dance*?"

Dangle: Deking around an opposing player.
    Example: "Jimmy *dangled* around the defenceman and took a shot on goal".
    Beer League Characters best represented: "The Puck-Hog" (pg. 54), "The Stud" (pg. 80)
    Classic Beer League expression regarding this term: "Where's your jock strap?"

Dirty goal: Deke through an entire team and fire the puck in the net, and you've got yourself a "dirty goal". The term "dirty" can be used for a number of on-ice events ie: "dirty move", "dirty deke", "dirty save". "Dirty" simply puts an emphasis on just how good a play was.
    Example: "The speedy forward scored a *dirty* goal to win the game".
    Beer League Characters best represented: "The Stud" (pg. 80), "The Ringer" (pg. 18)
    Classic Beer League expression regarding this term: "That's a *dirty* goal right there!"

Drop the mitts: A term used when hockey players engage in a fight. "Dropping the mitts" occurs when players throw their gloves down to the ice so they can begin their battle.
    Example: "Both players *dropped their mitts* and began throwing punches".
    Beer League Characters best represented: "The Goon" (pg. 24), "The Big Guy" (pg. 63)
    Classic Beer League expression regarding this term: "Ya wanna go? Then *drop your mitts*!"

Dummy: To beat up an opposing player as if they were a dummy or a doll.
    Example: "The big defenceman *dummied* his opponent ".
    Beer League Characters best represented: "The Chirper" (pg. 67), "The Goon" (pg. 24)
    Classic Beer League expression regarding this term: "That guy just got *dummied*!"

Face Wash: The art of rubbing your dirty glove in your opponents face. The "face wash" will often ensue when two player are mouthing one another off, but aren't exactly sure whether or not they want to fight. The "face wash" will annoy the hell out of players on the receiving end of it.
    Example: "The player received a *face wash* for poking at the other team's goalie".
    Beer League Characters best represented: "The Chirper" (pg. 67), "The Instigator" (pg. 70)
    Classic Beer League expression regarding this term: "That's a dirty *face wash*!"

Five-Hole: A term referring to the space between a goaltender's legs. Beer League players often shoot on this area of a goalie that doesn't go down much or a goalie that appears to be vulnerable in the net.
    Example: "The player skated in and went *five-hole* to win the game".
    Beer League Characters best represented: "The Sieve" (pg. 29), "The Angry Goalie" (pg. 62)
    Classic Beer League expression regarding this term: "You could've driven a train through there!"

Flashing Leather: When a goalie makes a spectacular glove save he essentially "flashed his leather" to stop the puck from going in the back of the net.
    Example: "The speedy forward tried to go high, but the goalie *flashed the leather* and made the glove save".
    Beer League Characters best represented: "The Wall" (pg. 47)
    Classic Beer League expression regarding this term: "Nice *flash of the leather*!"

Gongshow: Generally a term used after a night of chaos. A "gongshow" typically occurs after a hockey game, when players party to the extreme. The term may also be used if a game gets out of hand. ie; several fights, many penalties called.
    Example: "After the game, the boys were gearing up for another *gongshow*".
    Beer League Characters best represented: "The Story-Teller" (pg. 30), "The Drunk Guy (pg. 48)
    Classic Beer League expression regarding this term: "Get ready for a *gongshow* tonight, fellas!"

Gordie Howe Hat-trick: Simply put, you receive a goal, an assist, and get in a fight, and you've got yourself a "Gordie Howe Hat-trick". This expression was made famous by NHL Hall-of-Famer Gordie Howe, as he was notorious for receiving all three of these stats in a single game. The term lives on through rinks around the world and hockey of all levels.
    Example: "Johnny had a *Gordie Howe Hat-trick* last night".
    Beer League Characters best represented: "The Big Guy" (pg. 63), "The Stud" (pg. 80)
    Classic Beer League expression regarding this term: N/A

Horseshoes: Hockey is a game that can be full of lucky bounces, and tricky plays. Whenever luck happens to be on a player's side, opposing players will refer to him as having "horseshoes". Essentially "horseshoes" are a lucky item, like a four leaf clover, or a rabbit's foot. If a goalie makes a save without even seeing the puck, or if a player shoots a puck from a 100 feet away and it hops by the goalie, then those players are considered to have "horseshoes".
    Example: "That tender had *horseshoes* when he made that save!"
    Beer League Characters best represented: "The Pylon" (pg. 46), "The Seive" (pg. 29)
    Classic Beer League expression regarding this term: "That guy had *horseshoes* up his @$&".

Iron: Also known as the "Goalies Best Friend", the "iron" refers to the goal posts of a hockey net.
    Example: "The puck was shot off the *iron*".
    Beer League Characters best represented: "The Seive" (pg. 29), "Can't Buy One" (pg. 38)
    Classic Beer League expression regarding this term: N/A

Postage Stamp: Placing a perfect shot in the top right-hand corner of the net.
    Example: "The skilled forward put a *postage stamp* on that one!"
    Beer League Characters best represented: "The Stud" (pg. 80), "The Ringer" (pg. 18)
    Classic Beer League expression regarding this term: "Oooooooooooooh!"

Robbed: A play in which a player should have scored a goal, but the goalie pulled off a remarkable save.
    Example: "The goalie *robbed* him of a sure goal".
    Beer League Characters best represented: "The Wall" (pg. 47), "Can't Buy One" (pg. 38)
    Classic Beer League expression regarding this term: "Are you kidding me?"

Sauce: A great pass that is shot off the ice to a teammate's stick. The puck essentially looks like a flying saucer as it floats above the ice right on to his player's tape.
    Example: "The defenceman *sauced* the puck on to his forward's stick".
    Beer League Characters best represented: "Mr. Sportsmanship" (pg. 69), "The Veteran" (pg. 77)
    Classic Beer League expression regarding this term: "Nice *sauce*!"

Sin Bin: A term used for the penalty box. In order to head to the "sin bin", a player must have broken the rules, and received a penalty.
    Example: "The player's slashing penalty resulted in a trip to the *sin bin*".
    Beer League Characters best represented: "The Goon" (pg. 24), "The Angry Guy" (pg. 39)
    Classic Beer League expression regarding this term: "Take a seat, buddy!"

Snake Bitten: A term used to describe a player that is on a goal-scoring drought.
    Example: "George has been *snake bitten* for the fifth straight game".
    Beer League Characters best represented: "Can't Buy One" (pg. 38), "The Phony" (pg. 14)
    Classic Beer League expression regarding this term: N/A

Snipe: Another word for a goal. Typically you would refer to this term on a nice goal.
    Example: "Billy *sniped* two goals last game".
    Beer League Characters best represented: "The Stud" (pg. 80), "The Ringer" (pg. 18)
    Classic Beer League expression regarding this term: "Great *snipe*!"

Soft Hands: A player that is cool and collected with the puck is known to have "soft hands". Having soft hands means that you are a great stick-handler and have the ability to weave around your opponents with the puck with ease.
    Example: "The forward's *soft hands* allowed him to get around the defenceman".
    Beer League Characters best represented: "The Puck-Hog" (pg. 54), "The Stud" (pg. 80)
    Classic Beer League expression regarding this term: "Nice hands!"

Standing On Your Head: When a goalie is playing spectacular, he's known to be "standing on his head". Essentially, he's playing so well, that it's next to impossible to put the puck by him.
    Example: "The goalie is *standing on head* as he's already made 30 saves!"
    Beer League Characters best represented: "The Wall" (pg. 47)
    Classic Beer League expression regarding this term: "Somebody solve this guy!"

Stone Hands: A player that has trouble handling the puck is referred to as having "stone hands". Not only does this player have a tough time stickhandling and receiving a pass, but he also has trouble finding the back of the net.
    Example: "His *stone hands* have been causing him problems all game"
    Beer League Characters best represented: "Mr. Excuses" (pg. 25), "Can't Buy One!" (pg. 38)
    Classic Beer League expression regarding this term: *"Nice hands!"*

Tic Tac Toe: An expression used when several passes are made between players before scoring a nice goal. Typically the passes are all one-touch passes (in other words no stickhandling, just quick passes) before one of the players decides to shoot.
    Example: "The forwards just went *tic tac toe* to beat the goalie".
    Beer League Characters best represented: "The Stud" (pg. 80), "The Kid" (pg. 32)
    Classic Beer League expression regarding this term: *"Tic.....tac.....toe!"*

Twig: Another term used for a hockey stick.
    Example: "Terry brought out a new *twig* for this game".
    Beer League Characters best represented: All
    Classic Beer League expression regarding this term: N/A

Twine: Another word used to describe the mesh attached to a hockey net.
    Example: "The puck was shot hard and hit the *twine*".
    Beer League Characters best represented: "The Seive" (pg. 29), "The Angry Goalie" (pg. 62)
    Classic Beer League expression regarding this term: "Way to bulge the *twine*, buddy!"

(Going) Upstairs: Refers to a player shooting the puck and hitting the top of the net. This term may also be referred to as "roofing the puck", "top cheese", or "going cheddar". Most Beer League players love to shoot high, as it always looks better then firing it along the ice.
    Example: "Barry walked in and put the puck *upstairs*".
    Beer League Characters best represented: "The Stud" (pg. 80), "The Ringer" (pg. 18)
    Classic Beer League expression regarding this term: "Right where Grandma puts the peanut butter!"

Wheels: A word used to describe a player with exceptional speed. The term can also be used as a verb for a player to use their speed and skate as fast as they can.
    Example: "Watch out for that player – he's got *wheels!*"
    Beer League Characters best represented: "The Kid" (pg. 32), "The Try-Hard" (pg. 36)
    Classic Beer League expression regarding this term: *"Wheel! Wheel!"*

Acknowledgements

I WOULD LIKE TO THANK THE MANY PEOPLE INVOLVED IN MY LIFE TO MAKE THIS BOOK POSSIBLE. I WOULD ESPECIALLY LIKE TO THANK MY FRIENDS AND FAMILY FOR SUPPORTING ME THROUGHOUT THE MANY VENTURES OF MY LIFE. THIS INCLUDES MY MOM AND DAD - BOB AND JUDY, AS WELL AS MY SISTERS - TAMMY AND TRICIA.

THANKS TO MY BOYS I HAVE GROWN UP WITH AND HAVE PLAYED HOCKEY WITH FOR YEARS, INCLUDING KRAUSY, DREWPIE, PAGS, FAGEL, PHILLY, FRAZ, BBB, GARCIA, SIMON, LUCA, NARRYL, OPPS, ADS, O'DAWG, SCOTTIE, BRIDEN, JOHNNY C., AND STONEMAN, WHO ARE ALL AMAZING PEOPLE BOTH ON AND OFF THE ICE.

THANKS TO ALL OF MY NON-HOCKEY BOYS - CASH, ZUC, JT, CARM, JUAN, NARA, AND BURG. DON'T WORRY - WE'LL BE GETTING YOU GUYS OUT SOON!

THANK YOU ALIDA FOR EVERYTHING, PARTICULARLY PUTTING UP WITH MY LATE NIGHT HOCKEY TALK.

I WOULD LIKE TO THANK BOB SHERWOOD FOR HIS ENTHUSIASM AND CREATING FANTASTIC CARICATURES THROUGHOUT THE BOOK. YOU WERE A PLEASURE TO WORK WITH.

THANKS TO MY GOOD FRIEND JAMIE ROBINSON FOR HELPING EDIT THE MATERIAL OF THIS BOOK.

I WOULD ALSO LIKE TO THANK THE HUNDREDS OF PLAYERS I HAVE MET OVER THE YEARS WHICH ENABLED ME TO WRITE THIS FUNNY STORY OF THE BEER LEAGUE WORLD. THESE ARE THE PEOPLE THAT TRULY MADE THIS BOOK POSSIBLE.

IN CLOSING, I WOULD LIKE TO THANK EVERYONE ELSE WHO I MAY NOT HAVE MENTIONED. I APPRECIATE EVERYTHING YOU HAVE DONE FOR ME THROUGHOUT MY LIFETIME.

About the Author

STEVE DUNCAN WAS BORN AND RAISED IN GUELPH, ONTARIO, CANADA AND HAS A DEGREE IN JOURNALISM AND COMMUNICATIONS MEDIA. CURRENTLY THE LEAGUE COORDINATOR OF ADULT RECREATIONAL PROGRAMS, STEVE WAS INSPIRED BY MANY PEOPLE TO WRITE THIS BOOK WHILE RUNNING THESE LEAGUES.

ONE OF STEVE'S PASSIONS IS COACHING THE GAME OF HOCKEY. WITH OVER 10 YEARS OF EXPERIENCE, HE CURRENTLY WORKS WITH CHILDREN AND ADULTS OF ALL AGES, BRINGING THEM CLOSER TO THE GAME THEY ARE LEARNING TO LOVE.

STILL PLAYING IN BEER LEAGUE'S HIMSELF, STEVE REPRESENTS A FEW OF THE CHARACTERS DISPLAYED THROUGHOUT HIS BOOK. HOCKEY IS HIS PASTIME AND EVEN THROUGH THE TOUGH TIMES, HE CONTINUES TO CHEER FOR THE BOYS IN BLUE AND WHITE.

OFF THE ICE, STEVE'S FAVOURITE THINGS INCLUDE PLAYING BASKETBALL AND SOCCER, PARTYING WITH FRIENDS, SNOWBOARDING, WATCHING MOVIES, EATING FAST FOOD, EDITING VIDEOS, AND JUST PLAIN OL' HAVING FUN.

FOR MORE INFORMATION ABOUT THE AUTHOR OR THIS BOOK PLEASE VISIT WWW.BEERLEAGUEBOOKS.COM.

For more information about the artist,
please contact Bob Sherwood
cartoonbob@cogeco.ca (905) 659-5428